T0285513

The Greta Garbo Home

for

Wayward Boys and Girls

Also by Steven Gaines

Marjoe
Me, Alice
The Love You Make
Heroes and Villains
Simply Halston
Obsession
The Sky's the Limit
Fool's Paradise
The Club
Another Runner in the Night
One of These Things First

The Greta Garbo Home for Wayward Boys and Girls

a memoir

Steven Gaines

Delphinium Books

The Greta Garbo Home for Wayward Boys and Girls

For information, address DELPHINIUM BOOKS, INC.,
1250 4th Street 5th Floor
Santa Monica, California 90401
Library of Congress Cataloguing-in-Publication Data is
available on request.
ISBN 978-1-953002-42-6
Jacket and interior design by Colin Dockrill, AIGA

MY NAME IS JACK
Words and Music by JOHN SIMON
© 1967 WC MUSIC CORP. (ASCAP)
All Rights Reserved
Used by Permission of ALFRED MUSIC

For Tony D'Alessio

My name is Jack and
And I live in the back
Of the Greta Garbo home,
With friends I will remember,
Whenever I will roam
And my name is Jack,
And I live in the back,
Of the Greta Garbo home
For wayward boys and girls

—John Simon

PART ONE:

Sleeping With Women

I was twenty-three, lost and loose in Greenwich Village, 1969. I kept afloat as a worker at a downscale auction gallery in the East Village. At the end of each day, my $20 salary was paid by Ziggy Zazlow, the jolly auctioneer who peeled twenty bucks from a fat roll of bills he kept stuffed in his right pant leg pocket, which stuck out on his hip like a goiter. Antiques were a big cash business and I never once saw anybody write a check. My days at the gallery began with cleaning up the poop of Splat, the vicious watchdog and feral stray, named for the sound of his farts, and who sank his teeth into my ankle each day as I walked past his food bowl, once sending me to the emergency room at St. Vincent's.

Most mornings at the gallery I spent faking antiques from cheap Chinese import, softening the glaze with steel wool and motor oil. I also gently distressed furniture by dragging thumbtacks in a leather belt across the wood. On Saturday mornings the auctions were held at the gallery, but occasionally we held lawn auctions. Ziggy would drive us to a house on Long Island, where we tagged all the belongings of the owners who had died, or were moving to Florida, difficult to discern which, probably for them, too. It was sad to be foraging through the closets of other people's lives, going over their personal possessions, shoes, picture frames, the mattresses they slept on, assigning them a lot number. I wondered if one day my own life would be tagged and priced and sold off to strangers. Or worse, not.

I never felt like I had reached a dead end working at the auction gallery. I figured I was just passing through, treading water, waiting for my number to be called in the bakery of life to get a slice of fresh, hot opportunity. Only you really had to listen hard for that number in New York, a very noisy place with a lot of people clamoring for things. Anyway, I liked working at the shabby gallery with the tin ceiling. I enjoyed the whole carnie of it, the big Saturday auctions held in the main room with its assortment of oddball antique dealers, cloisonné collectors, and netsuke mavens who came every week to bid and buy. I especially enjoyed Ziggy Zazlow, with his silver-tongued spiel about antiques that perhaps were not. At the Saturday auctions, I helped carry "restored" furniture up and down the center aisle so people sitting in the folding chairs could get a closer look. If I helped carry the merchandise out to a van or car when the auction was over, I was happy to get a five-buck tip so I could get take-out shrimp and lobster sauce for dinner.

I wound up living this way after attending New York University film school, which left me expertly prepared to do nothing. Albeit an impractical education, it was a wonderful way to go to college, sitting in a dark theater every day, stoned, watching films that were explicated by a young instructor, Martin Scorsese, with whom I studied, and who had a secret student girlfriend I ended up sleeping with, much to his outrage—I had no idea they were involved. When he found out I had slept with her, he screamed at me as we met face-to-face waiting for an elevator on the eighth floor of the Education Building. I tried to assure him that I was innocent, that it was a one-off, and that the liaison lasted exactly as long as Procol Harum's "A Salty Dog," which played on her stereo, clocking in at 4 minutes and 33 seconds. Luckily for me, those four and a half minutes didn't seem to affect Scorsese's judgment as a teacher, because he still gave me an A on my final exam.

Yes, I slept with women. It was part of my homosexual cure with Dr. Wayne Myers, a talented Freudian psychiatrist whom I'd met at Payne Whitney, the time-worn but respected psychiatric clinic on Manhattan's Upper East Side. I was willingly incarcerated there at age fifteen after a serious attempt at self-annihilation involving windowpanes. I was a gay Jewish kid who lived in a thicket of self-hatred above his grandma's bra and girdle shop in Borough Park, Brooklyn, a *shtetl* twenty-five minutes by train and a chasm of erudition from Manhattan.

Dr. Myers, who was my psychiatrist at Payne Whitney, was touched by my deep despair and offered to help. Homosexuality was a psychiatric disorder, classified in 1952 in the American Psychiatric Association's first *Diagnostic and Statistical Manual of Mental Disorders*, as a "sociopathic personality disturbance." However, even Freud didn't believe that homosexuality was sociopathic, or that it could be cured, or should be cured. In his 1935 "Letter to an American Mother," he wrote to a woman who asked him to cure her son: "Homosexuality is assuredly no advantage, but it is nothing to be ashamed of, no vice, no degradation; it cannot be classified as an illness; we consider it to be a variation of the sexual function, produced by a certain arrest of sexual development. Many highly respectable individuals of ancient and modern times have been homosexuals, several of the greatest men among them (Plato, Michelangelo, Leonardo da Vinci, etc.). . . . By asking me if I can help, you mean, I suppose, if I can abolish homosexuality and make normal heterosexuality take its place. The answer is, in a general way, we cannot promise to achieve it. In a certain number of cases we succeed in developing the blighted germs of heterosexual tendencies which are present in every homosexual, in the majority of cases it is no more possible."

And so, when I was fifteen years old, we set out to reanimate the blighted germs of my heterosexual tendencies, hoping I would be one of the lucky few to succeed. The principal was that if we figured out why I was homosexual, then I wouldn't be one anymore. In the unraveling, the thing disappears.

There was just one catch. No sex with men. No masturbating about men. Each homosexual orgasm was a brick in the wall to my heterosexuality. The cornerstone of the cure was to deny my homosexual impulses and exchange them with copious coitus. Heterosexuality, it seemed, was an acquired taste, like scotch. The more sexual relations I had with women, the more I would learn to love the labia. Problematically, I had great difficulty bringing myself to experience labium firsthand. I had absolutely no interest whatsoever in exploring that part of a woman's body. In fact, the whole notion of the vagina made me wildly anxious. I may have spent more hours discussing vaginas with Dr. Myers than straight men have shooting the breeze in any locker room. My aversion to the vagina fascinated Dr. Myers. It wasn't just my attraction to men that was a symptom of mental illness, it was the "hysterical rejection" of the vagina, as he called it, for who would reject a vagina unless it was hysterical?

I never believed for a moment that Dr. Myers meant any harm. He was a good man. Why did I continue to cooperate in my cure even though I knew it was hopeless? Didn't I know, deep inside me, that I was hardwired gay? Of course I did. That reality crossed my mind a million times, but I fought it back, knowing that if I embraced the truth, it would mean spending the rest of my life on the fringes of society. As the years in analysis passed, I worried that I would be unhappy either way, as a closeted gay or as a fake straight. Norman Mailer, a writer whom I admired, wrote that the most respectable thing a homosexual man could do was not act on his desires. So I didn't. All therapy and no play makes Jack a very unhappy boy.

During this period, Dr. Myers's office was up on East 74th Street in one of those white bathroom tile, doorman buildings that had sprung up all over the Upper East Side. There was a simple waiting room, a blank white space with a few chairs. His sessions were fifty minutes with ten-minute intervals, so the waiting room was always empty. There was a set of back-to-back soundproofed doors that led to his office. Dr. Myers was in his early forties. He had blond hair, kind blue eyes, and he was a careful listener. He also had the unique talent to have a blank expression that was not judgmental, and yet seem interested and concerned. I didn't look at him very much, because I was in formal Freudian analysis, and every session I lay on my back on a beautiful leather divan, facing away from him to lessen his presence so I could free-associate without distraction. In front of me was a framed print of the center panel of Bosch's *Garden of Earthly Delights* hanging on the wall. This is the panel that depicts a paradise of lust, with lots of cavorting naked figures, including one with a flower planted in its anus.

I had a problem with the foot covering on the couch. Why was it there? Are you supposed to keep your shoes on or take your shoes off? I began to worry about how clean my socks were before I went for a session. Sometimes I took my shoes off, but not if I wore sneakers. When I finally screwed up the courage to ask him if I was supposed to take my shoes off, his response was, "What are your thoughts on having your shoes off?"

There was also an issue with rituals. Dr. Myers asked if I followed any specific pattern before therapy, and indeed, I had a slice of pizza before each session at Original Ray's Pizza up the block. I don't know if he asked me this because he smelled the pepperoni, but once I'd admitted to having a slice and a Coke before sessions, he asked me to stop. The sessions were at random times for a reason, he said, and he didn't want it to be part of a convention I had developed that might inhibit my free associating. I figured, "In for a penny, in for a pound," and if I was going to be analyzed, I better do it right, so I stopped having pizza, most of the time anyway.

Six years and $100,000 into analysis, nothing had changed. At twenty-one, I was a pressure cooker of testosterone. My head ached from priapism, and at times I felt like my eyes were bulging out of my head with bottled-up desire. Finally, Dr. Myers gave me an ultimatum: Either I took the plunge with a woman, or there was no sense continuing therapy. If I changed my mind about becoming straight, he would recommend me to another psychiatrist, whom, I assumed, would help me make the best of it while I wallowed in the swamp of homosexuality.

Shortly before I met Martin Scorsese's student girlfriend, I'd finally lost my virginity to a woman in a hotel room in Philadelphia. Two hotel rooms, to be specific. When I shared the impending loss of my virginity with a wealthy, older gay friend, he offered to pay for two adjoining hotel rooms in Philadelphia. The first room was for the actual penetration, if it took place; the second was for me to retreat in shame in case it didn't, where I would weep with humiliation at my failure.

I enlisted the help of a slightly older, pretty fashion illustrator of my acquaintance to take my virginity. Eileen was blond and blue-eyed, a Carnaby Street dolly via Queens. She was flattered to be asked to introduce me to the mysteries of a woman's body. While we talked about the possibility of fornication, she drew a sketch of me wearing a neckerchief, and left it to dry under her window air conditioner. Before long two drops of condensation fell on the drawing just where tears would have been under my eyes. When she showed it to me, I thought, "The Madonna weeps." I had a sign from God to get laid. It was *beshert*.

If consummation was my goal, then my lovemaking was a success, but of course, in reality it was not lovemaking. It was more like "show and tell." It mortified me to have my own body noticed and touched, although I responded like any twenty-one-year-old to oral sex. The fearsome vagina up close neither thrilled nor repelled. I was baffled. Given, I was a gay man, but still, I was expecting at least an alluring portal of sexual desire, a raison d'être that heterosexual men were so eager to put their dicks in there. It was okay if you liked that kind of thing, but truthfully, I didn't understand why God or nature didn't make it more appealing. Or maybe that was the point. Maybe it *was* appealing, but I was blinded to its beauty by my homosexuality? If vaginas are so beautiful, why aren't there more statues of them? Why is the meanest denigration when you call someone a cunt?

I was disconcerted by the array of new tastes and fragrances, and the occasional suction sound the vagina made during intercourse. I had never considered before that someone might pass gas during sex, and I was so uptight that I wasn't amused when it happened to her, and me. Cunnilingus, at which it turned out I excelled, was a dark and smothering experience, but it was thrilling to hear my partner respond with breathy little gasps that made me feel like I was fulfilling my male prerogative.

Cheered on by Dr. Myers, I became a serial affairist. It wasn't hard for me to meet young women; my *sub rosa* indifference was a turn-on. Since I approached the whole sexual thing as more of a tourist than a native, I became a connoisseur of the female body in the way a Jew appreciates the Vatican. It was a matter of honor to be a tender, satisfying partner, so I performed all the obligatory sexual acts in appropriate order. *Petit déjeuner, déjeuner*, and *diner*. But making love is not the same as lust. Even psychiatry didn't claim to know how to make people lust. And lust is the glue of love. Oh yes it is. At least at first. Over the years I had a lot of fun with women in bed, and some of it was passionate, but no matter how good it felt physically, it completely lacked *spurca libido*, Latin for "filthy lust." It's filthy lust that makes sex and love ignite. In my unseasoned mind, heterosexuals tried to find love and expected lust to grow. And gay men tried to find lust and hoped love would grow.

It was a depressing and guilty time for me. I was a cad. Many of the women I dated were sincerely in search of a lifetime companion and progenitor; when inevitably I moved on, it was heartache, sometimes for them and always for me. There were women I thought I could love, but not completely. I was hard wired to love a man more, and I was frustrated and furious with myself.

Then, just like in fairy tales, I was strolling down Columbus Avenue one April night when I was smitten with a girl I saw on the street. Smithy (not her real name, but an appropriate pseudonym) was laughing at something one of her friends had said, all of them fresh-faced Columbia grad students, pretty and smart women and handsome men, great white smiles and good hair, at the prime of their lives, none of whom would ever again be as beautiful as they were that spring night. I couldn't help myself from staring, they were all so striking, and Smithy saw me looking and I thought I could see from that quick glance she saw something in me, too. Or maybe she caught me staring at the guys too long, I don't know. I thought she was smashing and debonair, and it wasn't just the way she looked, it was her spirit and spunk, I could tell just from watching her walk down the sidewalk.

Whatever, I followed Smithy and her friends into one of the noisy Upper West Side Yuppie bars on Columbus Avenue. I ordered a vodka martini and stood near her group, stealing glances. After a few minutes of pretending I wasn't eavesdropping, she nodded to me over her friend's shoulder and I smiled. I felt such a tug. I went over to her, shy and embarrassed, and introduced myself. I couldn't think of anything to say, my usual glibness dried up.

"I like a martini with a twist guy," she said to me, toasting with her gin and tonic.

I liked her. She was a student at Columbia Law, and she intended to become a public defense attorney to defend the poor and downtrodden. She laughed when I said she should become a private attorney and defend the rich and unjustly accused instead. "There aren't that many rich people unjustly accused," she said. "It's usually the poor ones who get caught."

After we ordered a second round, she asked if I was gay. "I'm not gay," I said, trying not to look flustered. "Why, do I act like I'm gay?"

She gave me a skeptical look, so I invited her back to my ramshackle apartment to prove my manhood. I was prepared to roll out my well-rehearsed sexual repertoire; instead I went off autopilot and it was intense and dirty. I thought the top of my head would blow off. Out of nowhere, this happened. "Yup, you're right, you're not gay," she said as we were soaping up each other in the shower. She was correct. Those couple of hours I spent in bed with Smithy, I wasn't gay. I wasn't anything.

The next time I saw Smithy, she gave me a set of new sheets. "If this is going to continue, we can't have sex on Dudley Do-Right sheets," she said. I thought the Dudley Do-Right sheets were ironic, but I guess she didn't get the joke. She gave me a nickname, too, the first time I had a *petit nom d'amour*: "Cowhead."

"Cowhead," she called me, lying in my bed, tugging on my forelock when I couldn't remember whether George Eliot was a man or a woman. "You're too smart to be so dumb." She said it didn't matter to her that I moved furniture at an auction gallery to pay the rent, because she didn't think I'd be working there for long. She didn't say exactly where she thought I might be instead, but still, wasn't that encouragement?

So it was that after several months of dating hot and heavy, I was invited to meet her family at their home in Rye, where her father, Peter, who was a managing director at the marketing firm, JK Allen & Co., owned a house with a fireplace in every bedroom. On the way up on the train with Smithy, I fantasized about what would happen at dinner, how I would charm them into approving of me and I would become a part of the family, marry their smart daughter, and live happily ever after, financially cushioned by my rich in-laws.

Smithy's older brother, Tiernan, was waiting for us at the Rye train station. He was God's cruel prank, a *dybbuk* sent to remind me of what was really possible in my life and what was not. Just one look at him, standing at the curb next to the family's Saab station wagon, dressed in jeans and black ski parka with lift tags from Vail hanging by the zipper, I knew the whole weekend would be hell. Tiernan *was* Smithy, but as a man. He was twenty-eight, athletic, a graduate of UC Santa Barbara, a junior partner in a corporate law firm with fifty-two names. I was so deranged by my intense attraction that I couldn't raise my head for fear of gazing at him. To make things exquisitely worse, Smithy's demon younger brother, Colin, sixteen years old, pimply and mean, was on to my game and shot me sideways glances whenever his older brother entered the room.

Smithy's dad, "Call-me-Pete," played squash at the New York Athletic Club, because "tennis is for girls," he said, sipping McCallan's neat. He had primate hair on his knuckles, and I could see his overriding, square jaw in the faces of his handsome children. I wondered, if Smithy and I had children, would they have the boiled potato essence of my Eastern European stock, or the chiseled Anglo-Saxon features of the Smiths?

At dinner, Smithy's mother questioned my "Cowhead" nickname and Smithy told her that I was sometimes "absolutely brilliant" about things, and other times I was just a plain "Cowhead." Her mother nodded sympathetically at me. When Pete asked what I did for a living, I said I worked at an auction gallery.

"Sotheby's?" Pete asked.

"I'm afraid not, no," I said. I explained the more down-to-earth establishment I worked at. To be amusing, I thought, I told them about Splat the watch dog, and I explained how we faked antiques. The Smith family stared at me incredulously.

"Isn't that a crime, faking antiques?" Tiernan asked, cutting into a juicy steak.

I mumbled something about the antique gallery being responsible for how it represented its merchandise, not me as an employee.

"Oh, I don't know about that," Pete-the-lawyer said, shaking his head. "Not if you're knowingly involved in faking the merchandise."

I had a second glass of wine. Smithy's mom asked me if I was related to Charlotte Gaines from Arlington who was in her college graduating class in 1950. I said I wasn't, and I considered for a moment telling her that my family were Askenazi from Eastern Europe and that we'd chosen our family name from a car dealership on Flatbush Avenue, Gaines Oldsmobile, but thought better of it. When she asked what my father did for a living, I told her he was a child guidance counselor in a New York City high school, and she said that she "admired" that my father was a "civil servant."

"Indeed, except for the civil part," I cracked. It fell deader than a sparrow in a snowstorm.

Then death stopped by the table. I felt the rare steak I was chewing slide halfway down my throat just behind my Adam's apple and coagulate into a mass. I'd heard about this feeling, this moment, when the food won't go up or down, it's a solid block, and you can't take even the tiniest breath or exhale, and in a split second you know this is how you're going to die. I recently read a magazine article about people dying from choking on food. One of the Kennedys—Joan Skakel, Ethel Kennedy's sister-in-law—choked to death on a piece of meat in 1967.

I knew I had only a few seconds to ask for help, but nobody was paying attention. I abruptly stood up, pushed my chair backward, and when they all turned to look at me, I pointed to my throat. Smithy asked, "Are you choking?" Before I could even nod, her brother Tiernan jumped up, spun me around so my back was toward him, wrapped his arms below my rib cage, and pulled up with a mighty tug. The steak came shooting out of my throat like a shot put. It flew in an arc and landed on the white tablecloth near my host's salad plate. It was a disgusting half-chewed piece of rare meat. My first instinct was to scoop it up with my napkin so no one would have to look at it, but suddenly the strength went out of me. It was the oddest feeling, my legs had no substance and I started to sink. Big, strong Tiernan grabbed me under my arms and kept me standing while Smithy put the chair under me. There was a small dark spot on the front of my pants where I had peed in fright. I was sorry I hadn't died.

"You're as white as a ghost," Smithy said, offering me a sip of water. It took me five minutes or so just sitting in the chair to revive, during which time I apologized, about 100 times, and thanked Tiernan another 100 times, and died inside 1000 times.

"This is what a close brush with death will do to you," I lied to Smithy later, shivering at the Rye train station, waiting for the last train to the city. That night there was an early frost and I could just about see my breath, but it was shame that had given me the shivers, not the cold. Smithy linked her arm in mine and walked me over to a bench in front of the closed ticket booth and we sat huddled together in silence waiting for the train. "Do you know that I love you, Smithy?" I asked her.

"No," she said. "I didn't know you loved me." She tightened her grip on my arm and pulled me closer. "That's sweet of you to say, but there are all different kinds of love."

I always knew she was a clever girl. In another minute or two, the train came.

I dropped her off in a taxi at her apartment building near Columbia University, and I never saw her again. I called her a few times, but I could tell her heart wasn't in it. She was a girl who was going places and looking for a traveling companion. "I'll always have a special place in my heart for you, Cowhead," she told me a few weeks later, bidding me farewell on the telephone.

"Promise me you won't call anybody else 'Cowhead'?" I asked her. She promised she wouldn't, and I believe she kept her promise. I saw her twenty-five years later, still beautiful, a talking head on a cable TV news show. She was a public defender in San Francisco.

The Gourmet Rip-Off Artist

One day at the auction gallery a friend from NYU film school called to say there was a job notice on the eighth-floor bulletin board from a company called Gourmet Productions, which was looking for a director/editor of TV commercials. Nobody at the film school was interested. For the emerging *artistes du cinema* at NYU, it was heresy to work at anything as crass as making TV commercials. But not as crass as tagging the furniture of dead people, so I immediately called Gourmet Productions, in Great Neck, Long Island, to offer my services.

The man who answered the phone on the second ring was Herb Shtarker, who identified himself as the president of Gourmet Productions. When I told him I was applying for the job, he had but one question for me: Did I know how to operate a 16 mm, windup Bolex? It was a piece-of-shit amateur camera, and I didn't even know how to put film in one, but I wasn't going to get fouled up on details, so I said I did know how to operate a Bolex, figuring I could quickly learn. It seemed odd that a production company would be shooting TV commercials in 16 mm because they would look grainy and cheap on the air. When I asked what kind of sound equipment they were using, Shtarker said, "No sound. Sound comes later." I'd never heard of "Sound comes later," but what did I know about the complicated world of television commercials? The man offered me $60 a day—triple what I was getting at the auction gallery—and told me to be at his office in

Great Neck the next morning at 9 AM, ready to put in a long day.

That afternoon I fed Splat the watch dog and I told Ziggy that I had been offered a job directing television commercials, and I was quitting.

Ziggy nodded and smiled and peeled off an extra twenty from his big roll, as a going-away gift. "You're gonna need it. But I gotta confide in you," he said. "Chances are, you'll be back here before long."

I assured him that my services carrying furniture would not be available in the future.

The next morning, I arrived at Gourmet Productions offices in Great Neck to discover they operated out of three rooms in a cinderblock building behind a strip mall. I also discovered that Herb Shtarker was a zeppelin of a man, maybe 300 pounds, a Thanksgiving Day balloon with rosacea, who gave off a faint musty aroma. He was dressed in a jumbo blue shirt and enormous sport jacket, like a parachute of clothing had fallen on him. He smiled almost all the time; even his resting face was a smile, with rows of shiny white false teeth. His life was a vicious circle; he was a guy who was angry because he was obese, and who was obese because he was angry. Both the chicken and the egg were anger. Whatever was at his core, his goals in life were food, money, and Actress-Model, Miss North America, Betty Signoretti.

Actress-Model, Miss North America, Betty Signoretti, had big boobs and zaftig hips, like a World War II pinup. She was a nice woman in her early thirties (maybe), anxious to be liked and not disrespected for being the girlfriend of a repellent character. I was instantly fond of her, although I shuddered to think of her being intimate with Shtarker, who had recently given her a mink fur coat as a gift. When she proudly asked me to stroke her mink, I didn't think the long bristles were from any animal, but I kept my mouth shut. To please Shtarker, Betty Signoretti wore the coat of suspicious origin every day, no matter what the weather, over an outfit of hot pants and skimpy knit top. It was her uniform. I was told by Shtarker that, out of respect, Betty should regularly be identified with her full designation: Actress-Model Miss North America Betty Signoretti. I said it with gusto, because clearly it made her feel good, although I never found out where the suspicious Miss North America title came from. The Actress-Model part was genuine because Betty Signoretti starred in every commercial Gourmet Productions ever made.

This was how it worked: Shtarker's Gourmet Productions bought hundreds of minutes of early-morning, 60-second spots from independent stations like WWOR-TV, or WPIX-TV, at bulk-rate prices. He then resold the time, door-to-door, to small business owners all over the New York area, who were dazzled by the idea of seeing their establishment advertised on TV. He would offer to shoot a TV commercial for them on the spot, and it would be on the air in a week. There were no appointments with prospective clients. Shtarker and his crew just dropped in on business owners on a whim. "These people need a TV commercial," Shtarker would say, pulling into the parking lot of a hardware store. The clients could be anybody—a printer in Melville, Long Island, a truck driving school in New Jersey, an accounting firm in Staten Island.

I spent my first day, and many days after that, in the back seat of Shtarker's four-door, white Cadillac Seville, wedged between Shtarker's pint-size, younger brother, Allen, whose Right Guard deodorant wafted toward me when he stretched, and Shtarker's first-cousin, Stanley, a gaunt fellow with a skittish demeanor who, Actress-Model Miss North America Betty Signoretti whispered to me my first day, had only recently been discharged from the Veterans Administration psychiatric hospital.

In fact, I had taken Stanley's job, and he wasn't happy about it. Shtarker had been helping Cousin Stanley to get back on his feet after his stay in the Veterans Hospital by giving him the job of cameraman/director on the TV commercials. Unfortunately, they had "creative differences," although I can't imagine about what. I had been hired to take over, much to Stanley's steamy resentment. Stanley had been relegated to voice-overs and announcing, and it was a task he took most seriously, spending his time in the back seat of the car cupping his hand to his ear and reading aloud the headlines to ads in the newspaper. "*You can make big money driving a cross-country rig!*" Stanley would suddenly read aloud at which everyone would clap and say how professional he was.

"'Big money,' Stanley!" Shtarker cooed enthusiastically. "Those are the important words, 'Big money.'"

"*Big money!*" Stanley boomed, and we all applauded.

Shtarker was always hot and sweaty, so he kept the car air-conditioning on high no matter how cold it was outside. Actress-Model Miss North America Betty Signoretti cuddled next to Shtarker in her dubious fur and hot pants, singing along to songs on the radio while he burped and passed gas. "You promised you weren't going to do that anymore, Herb," she pouted.

"Can't help myself, honey," Shtarker protested.

After an hour of driving north, we saw a billboard for Brickman's Dude Ranch in Peekskill, New York, and Shtarker said, "Oh, let's go there." When we arrived in the parking lot of the Dude Ranch, we poured out of the car like circus clowns. By the time I'd caught up, Shtarker was in the front office demanding that the lady behind the desk summon the boss for a "once-in-a-lifetime opportunity." The owner, an older guy, leathery from working outdoors, dressed in his theme park jeans and cowboy shirt, came out of the back office and the two Shtarker brothers went to work on him like a tag team. For only $1,000, the man could buy ten minutes of airtime on a New York television station, with the opportunity to buy more airtime at only $50 each, Shtarker told him. He didn't mention that all these spots would run in the middle of the night. If the man didn't have a TV commercial, for only an extra $500, Gourmet Productions would film and produce a 30-second television commercial for him that would be his to use forever. Shtarker said they would make the commercial right then and there on the spot, no muss no fuss. Brickman's Dude Ranch commercial could be on the air as early as next week.

Then there was the extra-added bonus that all the commercials would star the internationally known Actress-Model, Miss North America, Betty Signoretti. Here Betty came forward and smiled sweetly. If that wasn't enough, the man with the camera (that would be me) was a nationally known director of TV commercials, and that Cousin Stanley was a professional announcer who would do the voice-overs. Here Cousin Stanley cupped his hand to his ear and intoned, "*Brickman's Dude Ranch!*"

I was stunned when the owner of the dude ranch wrote a check for $2,500 to Gourmet Productions. The ineluctable lure of being on television. We were taken out back to where there were a couple of scruffy acres with stables and nags, and several bunkhouses for guests, with names like Roy Rogers Roost, and dreary rooms with cowboy motif wallpaper. Since Actress-Model Miss North America had to be in every shot, I was told by Shtarker to "take pictures" of the bed with Betty Signoretti lying in it. I set up the camera on the tripod with Cousin Stanley hovering nervously to make sure I got it right, and I shot ten seconds of Actress-Model Miss North America alluringly stretched out in bed, pretend-sleeping. Next I shot ten seconds of Betty Signoretti standing alluringly in the doorway in her fur coat and hot pants. We moved on to the stables, where Betty Signoretti caressed a pony alluringly. Then I shot a few seconds of the Dude Ranch owner and his wife standing behind the front desk, smiling and waving at the camera, with Betty Signoretti checking out. No luggage.

Less than half an hour later, we piled back into the car and in celebration we went to have lunch at a roadside diner. We sat at a big round table by the window, the only conversation was about the menu, and when it came time for Shtarker to order, I listened in disbelief as he ordered three separate daily specials, each including soup and dessert. He asked that all three be served simultaneously—all the soups and entrées and desserts, all at once. When the food started to arrive at the table, crowding out the rest of our plates, Shtarker ate in a bestial frenzy, slurping food into his mouth. He knew it was disgusting, glaring around the table like a mean dog guarding his food, waiting for one of us to challenge him. Actress-Model Miss North America Betty Signoretti was oblivious; she could have been stoned on a beach somewhere, staring straight ahead at the waves as she chewed her food the same way she chewed her gum, with her mouth slightly open. When Shtarker had finished all his lunches, he licked his chops, wiped his cheeks, threw his crumpled napkin on top of his plate, and said, "I'm a gourmet. I like good food."

When the check came, Shtarker asked me for $5 for my burger. I gave him $6 and told him to give the extra buck to the waitress, which he probably pocketed.

We were soon back in the car looking for the next victim, which turned out to be Tex's Tire and Muffler Service. We poured out of the car in the parking lot and the Shtarker brothers pitched the dubious owner, who paced with his hands in the pockets of his greasy overalls. From the parking lot I could hear Cousin Stanley say, "*World famous Tex's Tire and Muffler*," and Actress-Model Miss North America Betty Signoretti made an appearance to show some leg under her fur coat. In another couple of minutes, the owner was writing a check. I wound up the camera and took 20 seconds of two mechanics replacing a muffler, while Actress-Model Miss North America Betty Signoretti looked on with concern— would the car survive? —and another 20 seconds of her smiling joyously at a white-walled radial tire. Somehow, Shtarker also walked away with four new tires for his Cadillac, the cost of which he said would be credited to any future airtime. There wouldn't be any airtime at all. I edited the film myself and I couldn't figure out which side was emulsion. The splices fell apart overnight, and Shtarker told me to throw it in the garbage and forget about it.

We also made a commercial for a truck driving school, in which Actress-Model Miss North America Betty Signoretti played a housewife begging her husband to find a job that would pay "Big Money." One of my favorites was for a telephone wake-up service, where a live person would call and wake you up every morning. Actress-Model Miss North America Betty Signoretti was both the cheery caller and the comfy sleeper, curled up in bed swathed in her fur coat like a blanket, yawning lazily when the phone rang and her other-self alerted her it was time to get up and face the day. It didn't seem to bother anyone that her mouth moved way before we heard her voice say, "Hello?" (Sound did come later.)

Amazingly, Shtarker finally landed an impressive client: Nathan's Hot Dogs. Shtarker sold Nathan's a package of 60-second commercials that would appear on every Mets home game broadcast on WWOR-TV that season. Nathan's was paying a lot more than Shtarker's usual hit-and-run clientele, and this was a big deal for him, his foot in the door to Madison Avenue. Everyone at Gourmet Productions was all puffed up about it. Unfortunately, instead of shooting at Nathan's in Coney Island, which was charmingly honky-tonk and always crowded, we shot at one in the morning at the Nathan's on the corner of 43rd Street and Broadway, right down the street from a movie theater showing *Pink Lips, Wet Desires*. This particular Nathan's was the most unsavory of all the stores in the chain, noisy and brightly lit with fluorescent lights to discourage junkies from hanging out.

Shtarker said he was going to invite a bunch of his friends to meet us there so they could be extras in the background. Except no one showed up, most likely because he had no friends. The place was empty. The only ones in attendance were his brother and Stanley, and Actress-Model Miss North America Betty Signoretti. After it became clear no one else was going to show, Shtarker gave me a fistful of twenties and told me to go out on the street and use the money to recruit random people as extras. They could earn $20 and have all the hot dogs they could scarf down. Of course, no average citizen was strolling around Times Square at two in the morning. A half hour later I returned with a several transvestites and junkies in tow, along with a couple of frightened German tourists. The junkies were in the finished commercial, mustard on their lips, heroin in their eyes, along with Actress-Model Miss North America Betty Signoretti in a mink coat proving that she could swallow a hot dog with a smile on her face. It was Shtarker's magnum opus. It ran during the Mets game. I knew when it would be on, and I watched it every time in fascination that this travesty was on the air.

One afternoon Shtarker told me to fetch Actress-Model Miss North America Betty Signoretti at her apartment building on the Upper West Side and bring her to a liquor store in Patchogue, Long Island, where we were shooting a commercial. Betty had half a dozen cartons of costumes and wigs she needed to bring. It seemed that she complained she was tired of wearing hot pants and a mink coat in every commercial, and she wanted a challenge as an actress. Shtarker had arranged for a professional costume supply company to send an assortment of wigs and costumes to her apartment, which we had to bring with us.

Betty lived in a modest one-bedroom apartment that Shtarker paid for in a housing complex. She was very proud of her apartment, and showed me around her "*bood-whar*," including the bathroom, which had a pink shower curtain and frilly skin exfoliators hanging from the showerhead. She was especially proud of the view from her bedroom windows. Her apartment was on the sixth floor of one of four identical slabs of buildings facing each other across a massive parking lot. Betty shut all the lights in her apartment to better show off the view. There were hundreds of apartments, the windows glittering and flickering with the light of TV sets, like pointillism. She stood next to me, pressing against me, and we kissed, at first softly, and then with a burst of enthusiasm. Almost immediately she began to slowly sink to her knees in front of me and grapple with my belt.

I lifted her by her arms, helping her to her feet. I said something like, "This isn't right."

"We have time before we leave," she said.

I cleared my throat. "It's not you. I'm gay."

Her mouth dropped open a little. "I never would have known from the way you kissed me," she said, looking confused.

"Well, I've been practicing," I told her.

This confused her even more, so I said we better get going

or we'd be late. I buried my embarrassment by busying my-self carrying boxes of costumes down to my Volkswagen Bug, which was stuffed to the ceiling. As Betty and I packed the car, I sensed that her confusion about me was transitioning to resentment. On the drive to the liquor store, I tried to make small talk, but she was in no mood, so we listened to music on the radio and were silent

The liquor store turned out to be a big booze supermarket in a shopping mall. There was aisle after aisle of every imag-inable kind of alcoholic beverage. The whole store was lit by harsh overhead fluorescent bulbs, which was disorienting af-ter a time and made me feel light-headed. The owner of the store was there with his wife and kids and in-laws, and it was clearly a big deal for them that the store was going to be on TV. Shtarker's team was milling around trying to look busy. At one point Cousin Stanley bellowed out something like, "*Fine wines and liquors!*" at which Shtarker assured the owner, "Practice makes perfect."

Betty and all the boxes disappeared downstairs to the base-ment, which we were now calling the "dressing room." A half an hour later she appeared dressed as a Spanish flamenco danc-er. Sort of. She was wearing a black-and-red dress with tiers of ruffles that she was tossing around like a can-can dancer, flash-ing her panties. I wound up the camera and Shtarker yelled "Action!" Betty held up a bottle of Spanish wine and made a face like she was being goosed. I waited for something else to happen, but nothing. Herb yelled "Cut!" and then there was a serious discussion if there wasn't anything Betty could do that was more Spanish-looking. It was decided she should purse her lips and snap her fingers. I guess they were think-ing of castanets. Then ten more seconds of filming of finger snapping and pursing and we took another break until Betty reappeared dressed as an Apache dancer wearing a beret, quite obviously with no underwear under her black leotards.

Shtarker yelled "Action," and Betty sipped French wine and threw her head back and forth like she was being throttled by an invisible hand. Then another long, long costume change, during which the liquor store owner opened a bottle of Jack Daniels and we all did some shots. Betty startled everyone by appearing in white face, red lipstick, and a black wig, dressed as a Geisha. Herb yelled "Action," and Betty went to town on a bottle of sake. Next Betty appeared in her trademark hot pants and coat of suspicious origin, with a ski cap on her head, holding a snifter. This was for an après-ski brandy.

As time passed, Betty's wigs went slightly atilt and I could see that she was having too many sips of the product. So were we all. The costumes and booze went on very late into the night until we had touched all seven continents and twelve nationalities, and I shot a record 200 feet of film. When it was all over and I was packing up, I saw Betty talking animatedly to Shtarker, who kept glancing at me. When she was finished, he stormed over, took the camera out of my hand, and shouted at me with garlic breath from one of his several dinners, "You came on to my girlfriend! You're fired!"

At least she didn't tell him I was gay.

The next day I went to the auction gallery and asked Ziggy for my job back. He looked up from a tray of jewelry wearing a jeweler's loupe and said sure, I could have my job back. "You don't even have to clean up after Splat anymore," he said. "Stupid mutt went out for a leak and never came back."

Well, at least one of us had escaped.

Emma's Kitchen

"Did you see that?" Feiden demanded, glaring at his windbreaker lying on the seat of the taxicab next to him. "My jacket tried to strangle me." Truly, it appeared in the shadows of the taxicab that the sleeve of Feiden's navy blue windbreaker somehow had wrapped around his arm, and when he tried to free himself, the other sleeve flew up and grabbed him by the throat. He struggled dramatically with the jacket before regaining control. "When I tell people these things happen to me, they don't believe it," he grumbled.

Feiden unwrapped a stick of gum and popped it into his mouth. "*Oy vey, l'anxieté!*" he sighed, staring out the window, his reflection appearing and disappearing in the window glass with the passing streetlights. We were on our way to the Bucket of Blood, which was what Feiden called the back room of Max's Kansas City. We were going there to have dinner and celebrate his optioning the new Larry McMurtry novel *All My Friends Are Going to Be Strangers*. It was a beautiful book about a loner's quest for belonging and normalcy. Feiden's eyes teared up when he read me a line from the galleys: "The door to the ordinary places was the door that I had missed. The door to Emma's kitchen, or to all such places. There would never be an Emma's kitchen for me."

We were originally going to celebrate with a Death Burger at Café Le Sarge—which was Feiden-speak for a hamburger at Sarge's Deli on Third Avenue—but when I went to pick up

Feiden at Bromleyville, which is what he called the Bromley, the apartment building in which he lived on East 37th Street, we lost track of time listening to tunes, which is what he called music. By the time we were ready to go out, Café Le Sarge was closed.

Feiden said we didn't have to go out; there was some left-over Chicken Lenni in the refrigerator that his Hebrew Goddess mother, the "Angel Clare" (a name taken from an Art Garfunkel song), had sent over earlier in the day. I had never tasted Chicken Lenni, a fabled Jamaican dish made by the Angel Clare's cleaning woman, Lenni. But when he opened the lid to the Tupperware, it looked like chicken with rice and beans. Feiden said that maybe it wasn't Chicken Lenni after all; maybe it was just Chicken Oreganato, which was his name for all other chicken dishes that weren't Chicken Lenni.

I'd met Feiden a year or so before in the back room of Max's Kansas City. He introduced himself on the pretense that I was someone he had met in Austin when he was a producer on a movie starring Charlotte Rampling, although Feiden hardly needed much pretense to introduce himself to anyone. He was an advocate without a passport, an influencer thirty years before the Internet. His only platform was the words, "You must." Feiden would say, "You must," and people would lean in and listen. He would name a book to read or a screening of a great movie, or a rock group that was about to break big. "You must," Feiden would say. He also knew who you must avoid. He also somehow, knew a lot of attractive young men. Warhol had allowed Feiden to print business cards that said "Andy Warhol Talent Scout" on them. Feiden used the card successfully to start conversations with handsome men, and the ones he seduced were taken to the Factory the next day to meet Warhol.

Feiden "took me up" as an acquaintance, which seemed odd, since he knew a surfeit of rich and famous people from which to choose a buddy. I was just a hired hand at a down-scale auction gallery. But we had one unusual bond. We both had "Dot syndrome," as he called it. The term was Feiden's abbreviation of the 1950s homosexual code phrase "Is he a friend of Dorothy's?" Like me, Feiden had spent a decade trying to cure his homosexuality in analysis. For years he saw Dr. Melitta Sperling, a Park Avenue Freudian with a German accent, whose disapproving gaze followed him for the rest of his life. "*Les yeux de Melitte*," he would murmur whenever he felt pangs of remorse for his sexual adventures.

To punish ourselves for being gay, Feiden and I would get stoned and listen to Harold's bitter speech at the end of *Boys in the Band* on an original cast LP that Feiden had the week after the show opened. "You're a sad and pathetic man," Harold says to his friend. "You're a homosexual and you don't want to be, but there's nothing you can do to change it."

Then we'd go to Max's.

Two blocks north of Max's, at Park Avenue South and 20th Street, the cab passed under a ruby red, pencil-thin laser beam, quivering with particles of soot and smoke. The beam emanated from a second-floor loft window. Tens of thousands of people passed underneath it every day for years, wondering what it was, until the New York Times ran a story explaining that it was a light sculpture called Laser's End by an artist named Frosty Myers. The beam was aimed two blocks south through a hole cut in the awning of Max's Kansas City, where it was caught by a small mirror, which bent the beam and sent it through the plate glass front window, penetrating the cumulus of smoke that hovered above the long bar, three deep with poets and painters, passionate and stoned, drunk and argumentative, and landed on the rear wall of the back room, where the beam shimmered like a stoned-out Star of Bethlehem.

While there was no velvet rope at Max's, there was a nasty little black woman with thick eyeglasses, known as Tiny Malice. Her real name was Dorothy Dean, and she had graduated Harvard with a BFA. In 1953 she became the first female fact checker at the New Yorker, but was fired by Wallace Shawn because her vicious wit cut too close to the bone, and because she was intoxicated by noon. She was frightfully drunk all the time, sitting on a barstool at the front door to keep normal people out, which she did with a simple "You don't belong here, get the fuck out."

The back room was located beyond the stairway to the second floor, beyond the phone booth and the small toilets, where the drag queens peed sitting down, past the swinging doors to the kitchen, where Julian Schnabel cooked club steaks for a time, and where the sous chef occasionally jerked off in the shrimp cocktail. The room was a windowless cul-de-sac, no more than 30 by 25 feet, with rough carpeting on the walls. Feiden had nicknamed it the Bucket of Blood, not just because there were corpuscle red tablecloths and red napkins, but because the ether itself was exsanguinated by the color from a sculpture of four tubes of red neon. After you were there a few minutes, there were no colors, only red. The regulars who sat in the corner booth below the sculpture—it was called Paranoia Booth because everybody in the place could see you—would sometimes stick their chewing gum on the neon lights, which mightily pissed off the artist, Dan Flavin, whose estate, thirty years later, sold a copy of the sculpture at Christie's for $662,000.

Max's was agar for people who lived outside of societal norms. The people in the back room weren't customers, they were denizens. It wasn't clubby, it was tribal. Strangers were repelled or killed. Anyone could sidle up to the big bar up front, with "butch idiots," as the back room people called them, but the back room was table seating only, and a back room table was a prime piece of real estate, over the course of one night passed on from lounge lizard to lounge lizard, guarding their tables like squatters.

The room was kinetic and rubbery, people bouncing off the walls, skittering table to table, drink to drink, drug to drug, ashtrays filled with endless smokes and bumming of smokes, an occasional hand job under a napkin, a blow job under a red tablecloth. There were poets, artists, alcoholics, drug addicts, speed freaks, misfits, mainliners, skin poppers, superstars, rock stars, occasional movie stars, psychos, lost souls, scions, broke writers, broken painters. There were drag queens who were like X-Men, dissolute heiresses, a baby elephant (once), Jane Fonda and Roger Vadim (once), Andy Warhol (almost never), and all the Warhol martyrs and superstars, many of whom were doomed to overdose or suicide. There were also waitresses with attitude, dressed in black micro-mini skirts, frequently without panties, sometimes with a Tampon string showing. On each table there was a small bowl of dusty white chickpeas that would break your tooth if you bit on one. Instead, the chickpeas were used as projectiles when a war of chickpea snipers broke out, like a low-key food fight in a high school cafeteria.

In retrospect, it sounds rather unsavory, *n'est-ce pas?* Where was the charm in any of that? Was Max's really a walk on the wild side, as Lou Reed sang about the crowd at Max's in the song of the same name, or was it just a high school cafeteria on drugs? How can people compare it to *Deux Magots.* Yet there it was, a bar, a destination, a *folle pensée* come to life.

Fortunately, when Feiden and I arrived, it was too early for Tiny Malice to terrorize us, but we were carefully perused by the owner, Mickey Ruskin, who wanted Max's to be a freak bar, not a gay one. Max's Kansas City had nothing to do with

Kansas, nor was there a Max—there are half a dozen conflicting stories about the derivation of the name—all of them with the same kind of randomness you might name a stray cat—but there was Mickey Ruskin. He was a most unlikely salonist, a big shlumpy guy in ill-fitting clothes, grizzled, stringy hair that could have used a good washing. He had a chipped front tooth covered in a fuck-you, gold crown so he looked like a Jewish pirate when he smiled. If he ever smiled. Mickey was a legend, well-deserved. He was a Cornell-educated attorney who had given up the law to buy a threadbare coffee shop in the East Village. It was there that he nurtured a bohemian clientele of threadbare poets and painters. A few coffee shops and one restaurant later, Mickey opened up Max's, which somehow morphed into this petri dish of art and pop culture, poetry, gender experimentation, and drugs.

From the start, Mickey let his regulars run up tabs when things were tough, and they paid him with their poems, and their paintings, now probably worth tens of millions of dollars if he had hung on to them. One of my favorite pieces of memorabilia from Max's is a bill dated November 30, 1969, for $774.33 sent to Warhol at the Factory when it was on Union Square, from which Mickey deducted $200 for a Marilyn Monroe silkscreen.

When Feiden and I arrived at Max's, the back room was half empty. He ordered the *spécialité de la maison*, a club steak, "burned like Hitler's ovens," he told the bewildered waitress, and a *greps* tonic. He was commonly "mal de stomach," and any number of smells and tastes could disgust him. When the waitress placed the cherry Coke he'd ordered in front of him, he looked at it with suspicion, as if the straw might somehow attack him like his jacket had done.

"There's the new manager," Feiden said when a handsome young man in a dress shirt and slacks led a middle-aged couple through the room to the booth behind ours. When the couple immediately tried to order drinks, the manager said, "The waitress will be right with you."

"I think Tennessee Williams just sat down behind you," Feiden said.

"Sure thing."

"I mean it. He's with that woman he's so close with."

"Sure thing," I repeated.

"No, I *mean* it," Feiden said. Impatient with me, he reached across the table, and before I could stop him, he grabbed my fork and tossed it on the floor, where it landed with a terrible clatter. I was mortified. "Pick it up," he said.

I leaned over to pick up my fork and saw Tennessee Williams ordering a drink from the waitress.

"I can't believe it," I whispered to Feiden.

"Get up and introduce yourself," Feiden egged.

"Why would I do that?"

"Go introduce yourself! Ask what brings him here. Ask him what he's doing at Max's at this ungodly early hour."

"Why would I do that?"

Feiden rolled his eyes. "*You would do that to meet Tennessee Williams.* Have you no sense of adventure?"

Ten seconds later I was standing next to Tennessee Williams's table.

"We asked for some water," the woman sitting across from him said to me. She was a tiny person with a pointy nose, dressed in a beautiful black suit. This was the prickly Lady Maria St Just, Tennessee Williams's *amitié amoureuse*, and the inspiration for Maggie the Cat in *Cat on a Hot Tin Roof*.

"Oh, I don't work here," I apologized, humiliated. "I'm sitting in the booth behind you and I wanted to meet Mr. Williams."

"Were you eavesdropping, then?" Lady St Just asked.

"Oh no," I said. "It's just that Mr. Williams's voice is unmistakable." I turned my attention to him. "I'm such a big fan," I said. "When I was fourteen years old, my parents took me to see *Sweet Bird of Youth* on Broadway, with Paul Newman and Geraldine Page."

"Age fourteen!" Williams guffawed behind a cloud of cigarette smoke. "And was it transcendent? Did it bring you closer to Christ?"

"No, but it brought me closer to homosexuality," I said.

"Hah!" Williams barked, like an old pump rifle going off.

"How's that?" Lady St Just demanded of me. "How did it bring you closer to homosexuality?"

"I suppose that gay men are afraid they're going to end up like Alexandra del Lago." Del Lago is one of Williams's great viragoes: an aging, lonely, washed-up actress who shacks up with a handsome young actor who thinks she can further his career.

"Why is that?" Lady St Just persisted. "Why would gay men end up like Alexandra del Lago?"

"Youth and beauty fade, just like movie stardom, and you wind up wrinkled and lonely, lusting after young men," I said.

Tennessee seemed a tinge annoyed by this cursory analysis. "Well, Princess Del Lago is not here tonight," he rasped, exhaling cigarette smoke. "No ghosts. In fact, *nobody* is here tonight. This place is like a cemetery. Where *is* everybody? Where's Andy Warhol?" I guess he thought Warhol practically lived in the back room, but the truth was that Andy was segueing from druggies to society ladies, and he went to Max's only on an occasional whim, like a hajj, to keep the myth going.

Now Feiden, who had been practically crawling over the banquette dying to join the conversation, was standing next to me. He introduced himself as a movie producer and bowed from the waist like an orchestra conductor. When Lady St.

Just asked the nature of our relationship, Feiden with a straight face said, "Leopold and Loeb."

She looked at Williams and he looked back at her. "Then you must sit with us," she said.

Presently, the back room began to fill with a collection of curios, which delighted Williams. When Paul Morrissey, the director of most of Warhol's films, arrived, I was asked to go back to my booth so he could sit with them. A parade of otherworldly characters passed by to kiss Williams's ring, while I ate my cold cheeseburger alone and watched.

Later on, a woman with scraggly blond hair and Cleopatra kohl eyes, evidentially on a mix of Seconal and psychosis, climbed up on a table holding an empty Coca-Cola bottle and cried out "Showtime!" eliciting a round of hooting from the crowd. She pulled up her skirt and tried to insert the Coke bottle through a tear in her panties, to cheers and applause. "Showtime" was a spontaneous piece of performance art indigenous to the back room with the instigator standing on a table, and usually included a moment of nudity. The woman standing on the table that night began to sing an unintelligible song, drowned out by laughter and shouts, when Mickey Ruskin rushed into the back room, looking like he was the high school principal who caught students smoking in the bathroom. If Mickey caught you standing on a table doing Showtime, he put you in detention and banned you from Max's for a couple of days, or weeks. But if you were a regular, he would always relent. Mickey dragged the woman off the table and the crowd booed him affectionately.

Suddenly it was 2 AM and Paul Morrissey, Williams, and St Just vanished. All that was left were Feiden and me and the speed freaks. "You must come to the Factory with me tomorrow," Feiden said. "Paul Morrissey is going to screen his new movie for Tennessee, and I can bring you as my guest."

"How exciting!"

"Well, you deserve it. You went over and introduced yourself. You can never be too thin, too rich, or too forward."

Outside, the rain was so fine, it was like a mist. I looked up and down Park Avenue South, and there were fairies dancing in the air and the streetlamps had halos.

"You take the first cab," I told Feiden. "I want to walk home."

"Tomorrow at noon," he said, stepping out into the street, hailing a taxi by shouting, "Hearse! Hearse!" As the cab pulled away I knew exactly what his plan was. He was telling the driver that before taking him to Bromleyville, he should stop at an all-night newsstand on East 53rd Street, where Feiden would buy every magazine and newspaper that he hadn't bought the day before. He would spend the rest of the night listening to "tunes" and reading. If the phone rang, he'd let the machine pick up. Early in the morning, the dawn menacing him from behind closed blinds, he would retreat to the "coffin room," where he would read book galleys and film scripts in bed, dozing on and off. The elusive sleep for which he so longed, which he anthropomorphized as "Haughty Dame Poof," would never visit.

The next day I called in sick at the auction gallery and went to the Factory on Union Square for a screening of Warhol's new movie *Trash*. It took me about an hour to get dressed and comb my hair, and when I got to the Factory I might as well have been a ghost. I was scared to death, too nervous to make conversation in the event anyone acknowledged my presence, and even if anyone did acknowledge me, I had nothing to say. I clung to Feiden's side, and I managed to murmur hello to Warhol, who looked powdered and embalmed and bemused with me for a second, before he got bored with me and moved on.

The event was simple, no screening room, just a projector and some folding chairs in a big loft with the blinds closed.

The lights were turned off, a projector clattered, and whatever it was that appeared on the screen was just awful. The dialogue was incomprehensible, and the drag queens with bad teeth and sores on their skin were hard to watch. When the film was over, Williams raved about what he had just seen, along with Feiden, who called it "art." Feiden had previously been invited to stay for lunch, but I was clearly not included. I made some excuse that sounded like I couldn't stay even if I was asked, and I left.

Out on the street, it was amazing to think, Andy Warhol, Tennessee Williams, and me. I relived every second of it in my mind a thousand times. What Tennessee said, what Warhol said, what I should have said. I couldn't wait to tell people about the experience, but there was hardly anybody I knew who was interested. At Max's everybody knew Andy or somebody. The people at the gallery could care less about Warhol, or didn't believe me, and I don't think anybody there really knew who Tennessee Williams was. When I called my mother in Brooklyn, desperate for someone to be impressed, she was instead alarmed, because she heard Andy Warhol did drugs.

The Greta Garbo Home

I was living variously from short-term rental to short-term rental, my clothing in a suitcase and cardboard box. I wasn't making enough money at the gallery to pay steady rent, so sometimes I sofa surfed. For my mother and father in Brooklyn, the way I was living was one step ahead of being on the street. They wanted very badly for me to move back home to my trapezoid-shaped bedroom that had been cobbled out of the dining area with a flimsy wall. My parents had left the flat above my grandmother's bra and girdle store and moved to a one-bedroom apartment in The Sutton, a spanking new, white-tiled apartment building on Ocean Parkway. The Sutton was fancy for Brooklyn; it had a fancy name written in gilt script above the front door, it had doormen, it had a swimming pool on a sliver of land out back, and it was on Ocean Parkway, the most prestigious boulevard in all of Brooklyn, the Jewish Park Avenue, designed by Frederick Law Olmsted and Calvert Vaux, the men who designed Central Park. Yet perhaps its greatest distinction was that the fourteen-story Sutton was built directly next to Washington Cemetery, a vast Jewish graveyard that stretched out for blocks of ancient white headstone and gated mausoleums like little granite mansions.

My parents had lived in that building for six years, enough time so that my father wasn't talking to most of the other residents, plus the super and the doormen. He was the king of grudges. Because he didn't want to thank the doormen for holding the door open for him, he used the service entrance to enter and leave the building. All I had to do was mention an apartment number to him, 7B, for example, and my father would launch into a diatribe of resentments against the occupants. My mother, as usual, was steady as she goes, a calming presence to my father's storm. Once a week I went to Brooklyn to have dinner with them in the claustrophobic dinette wallpapered with a gold and orange-metallic amoeba design that made the room swirl just sitting still. Each visit I went to my old bedroom, and through my windows, beyond the cemetery, a few miles to the north, I could see the distant skyline of lower Manhattan, so romantic and ominous, calling to me like the Sirens, and I knew I could never move home again.

In June of 1970, I was driving down Seventh Avenue in my beat-up, pea green Volkswagen Bug, weaving in and out of traffic near the big intersection at 34th Street and Seventh Avenue, when I saw a young woman popping out from between two parked trucks, wriggling her fingers at people driving by, then popping back in. It took me a second to realize that she was hitchhiking, which was odd enough in New York City, where no one ever hitchhikes, let alone hitchhike by wriggling your fingers instead of putting out your thumb. I could not know that this was fate wriggling its fingers at me when I stopped and offered her a ride. That moment was the seed of my financial security for the rest of my life.

Her name was Phoebe, and she was a post-hippie flower girl in her early twenties, with beaded bracelets, thick rimless glasses, and long folk-singer hair tucked behind her ears. She worked for a messenger service, she said, hitchhiking home to West 11th Street in Greenwich Village to save the subway fare. It seemed pretty extreme to me, but she explained that she and her boyfriend, a struggling artist, were scraping together money for a six-month trip to Arizona, where they wanted to live in the desert and take peyote. They were searching for someone to sublet their apartment, a duplex with a garden in a townhouse, but all of their friends were too poor to afford it. She said they wanted $275 a month. Even by 1970 standards that was way too cheap for a duplex in a townhouse, so I asked if I could see it when I dropped her off.

146 West 11th Street was a little brick building, paint peeling, only 19 feet wide, built circa 1822. The apartment itself stank of patchouli oil and cat pee, and the linoleum that covered the floor was yellow and cracked. There were still outlets on the walls for gaslights, and the electrical wiring was copper wrapped in cloth. What had once been an outhouse—a tiny shack attached to the back of the building—had been jerry-rigged into a bathroom. This attached outhouse had no heat, and when it got cold in the winter, you had to burn a light bulb under the sink to keep the pipes from freezing. Even the view out the back was dreary—a weedy patch of city scruff, hidden from the sun by the house next door, hemmed in by the soot-covered cinderblock back wall of a gay bar on Greenwich Avenue. The front bedroom's windows looked out on the legs of people walking by.

I jumped at it. I signed a one-year lease with Phoebe's boyfriend, a congenial man named John Brody, and moved into the apartment on Independence Day, July 4, 1970. Within a few days, the view from the bedroom window that I'd found so dreary was now a glorious cityscape to me, romantic and destiny manifest.

There was one major caveat from John Brody: The owner of the building must not know I was living in the apartment, because if he found out, I would be thrown out for certain, but that I shouldn't worry much, because in all the years Brody had lived there, the owner had never come around once. This kind of illegal subletting thing was going on all over the place in the 1970s, and I was such a vagabond that although the uncertainty of subletting illegally didn't thrill me, it was only for a few months, and the worse that could happen was that I would be evicted and have to move again.

I wasn't living in the apartment an hour when the man and woman who lived in the apartment upstairs knocked on my door. They were authentic 1950s Greenwich Village Bohemians who wrote cookbooks and nipped at the brandy all day. They were full of neighborhood gossip and asked if I knew I was renting from a "squatter." It turned out that Mr. John Brody was the grown son of a couple whose lease had run out decades ago, and Brody was legally entitled to stay on month to month as long as he lived there and continued to pay the rent, which was $126.00 a month for the *entire* building. I guess that was a fair price when they signed the lease in the 1930s. I found this news fascinating, but I failed to see its true significance until six months later John Brody wrote saying he was moving to Japan, and would I like to stay a year longer?

I renewed my lease with him for a year by mail, and not long after, I went to the Municipal Building to look up who actually owned the building. His name was Victor Emmanuel and he was a Manhattan attorney. I found his number in the phone book and called his office. I explained to his secretary that I was living in the house he owned on West Eleventh Street, and asked if I could come to his office to discuss the building with him. The very next day, spiffed up in my tie and jacket, I was seated across his desk from him. Emmanuel, in his early seventies, was a courtly gentleman, from another time. He said that the townhouse was an "albatross." The ownership of the building had passed through many hands over the last 150 years, including most recently a church, and Emmanuel was given the townhouse in lieu of a fee in the settlement of an estate. He had no interest in it. It was ramshackle. And it was in debt. The unpaid New York City property taxes were piling up on the building, over $60,000 worth.

I explained that although I was only twenty-four years old, I felt a kindred spirit with the house. I had been there only a few days when I knew I was a part of it, somehow that was my home, and I didn't care how ramshackle it was. His squatters were gone; they had abandoned the property. He could legally evict them. I was proof, I had a signed lease. I asked that in return, Emmanuel net-lease the building to me for five years, with an option to buy, for the taxes due.

I don't know why he said yes. I think he just liked me; I was twenty-four years old, earnest, and starting out. I loved the city. My enthusiasm for the building was heartfelt. Perhaps he, too, could see that I belonged there.

Six weeks later, after John Brody had been legally evicted, I signed a deal with Victor Emmanuel and started patching the walls and painting the apartment shades of sand and paper bag brown with a single navy stripe along the moldings. I tore up the linoleum and scraped together whatever furniture friends and family donated. The people upstairs left and I moved a tenant into the upstairs apartment to cover expenses.

So now I had a duplex with a garden in the West Village. The stage was set. For what? I don't know. There was something . . . Tennessee Williams about it.

Tadzio

One of those red nights at Max's I ran into a young woman I knew, Caitlin. She had blond hair and brown eyes, a cotton-candy girl, endearingly shy, who spoke just over a whisper, anomalous considering she was a porn actress. She was pretty full-throated when she had an orgasm. I knew this because we'd met a few years before when I was rooming with three other NYU film school students in an immense, two-story, rat-infested loft on Greene Street in SoHo. The former factory was eighty feet wide and went through the block, all the way from Greene to Broadway. We decided to cover our living expenses by renting out some of the space as a studio for low-budget filmmakers, and the loft soon turned into a popular location to shoot straight porn movies.

So it was that I became inured to the sound of flesh smacking against flesh, followed by exaggerated fake orgasms. I was able to stand up in my sleeping loft with my head a few feet from the tin ceiling and watch the movies being shot below. The film crews often used our living room sofa as a prop, on which we had sprawled the night before, watching *Star Trek* reruns and eating s'mores. Sometimes the porn actors and actresses, in their loosely tied bathrobes, would wander over to the kitchen and have coffee with the NYU film students, and at one of these cozy breakfasts I met Caitlin, whom I had just watched from my sleeping loft while a muscular, olive-skinned man fucked her from several different angles. After toast and tea, I offered to show Caitlin my loft bedroom, where her loosely tied robe fell open, my underwear disappeared, and we had five minutes of unforgettable oral sex before her break was over and she needed to go back to work. I guess she had what you'd call a busman's holiday.

Dr. Myers was thrilled when I reported this quickie. He loved the naughty boy stuff, although he pointed out that I had just seen her having intercourse with a man with a large penis, and I admitted that had sharpened my desire. However, it sounded to him as if maybe I was really getting into the swing of things, and he encouraged me to see her again despite Caitlin being a porn actress, even if she wasn't the kind of girl I could bring home to my mother, as long as she had no venereal disease.

I invited Caitlin to have dinner with me the following week, and suddenly, dressed in street clothing, sitting in a Greenwich Village restaurant, she wasn't appealing to me anymore. I guess I was turned on by the whore, not the person. The atmosphere turned strained, and I asked her a whole bunch of geeky questions like, "How did a nice girl like you?" (Caitlin gave me some flower power rationale about love being free and that it was God's gift and that nothing was wrong with getting paid if people liked to watch her.) And "Does your mother know?" (Her mother knew and didn't care.) Caitlin was so sincere that I didn't challenge any of it. We didn't go to bed that night; we said goodbye on the street corner. But I liked her, and I was glad when I saw her sitting in the back room of Max's Kansas City a year or so later, along with a big, handsome outlaw named Floyd.

Floyd, twenty-one, was a blond, green-eyed dope, with a disarming, chipped-tooth smile and a beautiful body governed by a robust libido. Mythically handsome, you knew he was doomed. The principles in Baba Ram Dass's book *Be Here Now*, combined with the lyrics of the popular Stephen Stills song "Love the One You're With," constituted his *philosophie de la vie*. Which was just fine with me. He was so long and tall, he looked stretched out. He was wearing jeans and a blue Oxford button-down shirt with the sleeves rolled up. His hair, parted down the middle, flounced around his head, like an Afghan hound just coming from the groomer. Indeed, not unlike that of a puppy, he had a charming eagerness to be liked. When he picked up his wineglass, I saw that his hands were large and masculine, and his nails were clean and clipped. All of this Ken doll stuff would have been repellent if it was artifice—if his hair had been cut by a stylist, or he'd worn contact lenses to make his eyes greener, or if his teeth had been straightened. But no, Floyd was authentic, a twenty-one-year-old at the peak of his physical beauty as a young man, ripe with testosterone.

"What do you do?" I asked.

"There are two things I do really well," he said with a sly smile. "One of them is rolling joints." He didn't have to say what the other thing was. Pheromones wafted across the table toward me.

Tadzio, welcome to Max's Kansas City.

I felt like Puck had put love potion in my eyes. I looked at him like I was a cartoon character with hearts orbiting around my head. I was smitten. Floyd could tell, Caitlin could tell, the waitress could tell. Caitlin looked embarrassed for me. I stared goofily into his emerald eyes that held an empty universe, and listened enrapt as he told me that he had flunked out of Fairleigh Dickinson University in New Jersey and he spent the past summer working for a landscaper, mowing lawns to earn pocket money.

Two hours of covert flirting later, the three of us were drunk. I paid the check, and we walked outside and stood on the sidewalk. There was a clumsy pause until Caitlin suggested we all go to my house, so we hailed a cab and went to 11th Street. I opened a bottle of wine, and I put Joni Mitchell's dreamy *Blue* LP on the KLH. We smoked a joint at the dining room table, and we did some coke that Floyd had with him in a little origami folder fashioned out of a glossy page from a fashion magazine. Caitlin went downstairs to the bathroom, and when she was gone for what seemed like a long time, Floyd offered to go see if she was okay. I waited a few minutes until I realized he had disappeared too, so I crept down the staircase far enough to see through the door of my bedroom. A slice of light from the hallway fell across my bed. I could see Floyd lying on his back with his long, hairy legs draped over the edge, his pants and jockey shorts around his ankles. He was smoking a cigarette, lazily blowing smoke rings at the ceiling. Caitlin, naked, kneeled in front of him. I sat on the steps and watched for a while, dumbfounded and thrilled. Floyd must have known I was there because after a time he raised himself up on one elbow and said, "Hey, man, I hope you don't mind we took advantage of your bed."

In the safety of the shadows of my room, I was surprised by how easily it flowed, liquid and smooth. Floyd and I directed our attention to Caitlin, and I pretended that any physical contact with him was incidental, not electrifying. There was one particularly potent moment when we were inside her in tandem, and in the pitch black I could see him smiling at me. Until that moment, his face so close to mine, close enough to kiss, until that moment I couldn't comprehend what it was like to be consumed with lust, why lovers kill rivals, why lovers kill each other. I began to chase the emotional and sexual high of that triad, for decades to come.

They fell asleep in bed next to me, but I was too keyed up to shut my eyes. I lay perfectly still on my side for a long time, studying the man and the woman in bed with me, the lines of their bodies under the sheets becoming clearer with the gray morning light. I watched the way they breathed in their slumber, the peace on Caitlin's face, well drugged and properly fucked, and the perfectly formed shape of Floyd's slightly parted lips, like a baby's lips forming an *o*, the lawnmower boy at peace.

We got up the next afternoon around 1 PM, and had another lazy round, then a giddy brunch at a Village café. I was feeling wicked and thrilled with myself. When it came time to say goodbye on the sidewalk, we exchanged phone numbers, and Floyd said, "See ya, Glen." We each went our own separate ways. I went back to the townhouse and sat at the dining room table and looked around the empty room and cried. For what I was not sure.

Dr. Myers, who was by now long bored with the indeterminable limbo of my sexual identity, was positively reanimated by my *ménage à trois* with Floyd and Caitlin. Didn't I recognize that this was the re-creation of the seminal trauma that caused my homosexuality—watching my mother and father have sex when we shared a bedroom when I was a child. Only now I wasn't left out, crying and fearsome in my little bed. Now I had joined my parents.

He really knew how to squeeze the fun out of everything.

He also pointed out that although there was a woman present, I was really having sex with Floyd, not her. Dr. Myers strongly suggested that I not have any further contact with Floyd, before I went down a path from which I could not turn back.

I called Floyd the next day to say that if he ever needed a place to stay in the city—and no more words came out of my mouth before he interrupted, "Sure. Can I stay over tomorrow night?"

He held my complete attention. I stopped thinking unless it was about him. I didn't work, I didn't want to, it would disrupt my pursuit of Floyd. Floyd didn't so much as move in with me as he didn't leave for weeks at a time. Occasionally he would go to New Jersey to retrieve some of his possessions, although he didn't seem to have many belongings, except for a handful of jeans and sweaters, his sheepskin jacket, torn at the shoulder, like Leonard Cohen's "Famous Blue Raincoat." He also had a beat-up old motorcycle that was sad. His helmet, on the table by the front door, covered in a grime of exhaust and dead bugs was a trophy to me.

Floyd was once paid for an ounce of cocaine with a stolen Nikon and he decided he would become a fashion photographer, so I turned the downstairs hallway into a darkroom for him and introduced him to everyone I knew in the fashion industry, about two people. When he went out to buy drugs, I rummaged through his negatives to see where he'd been, which turned out to be mostly with his girlfriend, Ellyn, in a New Jersey condo, to which he would elope every few weeks to be drained of precious bodily fluids to the point of dehydration. Then a few days later he'd return to 11th Street to deal more dope and tell me about his copulations with Ellyn.

There were moments in this self-inflicted masochistic torture when it was the way I thought I wanted it to be, him having the girlfriend in New Jersey, him and me in the Manhattan townhouse smoking dope, watching television and eating Chinese. Then later, with Eric Clapton's "Layla" playing for the thousandth time on the KLH in the living room, I would go to his bed, where he would light a cigarette, lie back and smoke, and become a passive accomplice to a sex act which, despite his protestations, he was able to surrender to just fine, about the time Duane Allman and Eric Clapton's stirring guitar *pas de deux* finished. There were times also when we went out to a bar and picked up a woman together. We were a good tag team. I was hairy and Semitic and smart; he was tall and dumb and blond. The easy fluidity of his sexual response in bed, an exotic bisexual creature, fascinated me. He never showed me any affection, nor did I care, except at the odd moments when he was feeling soft, he called me "Glen." I have no idea why.

He was a jerk and he had ultimate control over me. And I was furious with him because of it.

Dr. Myers hated Floyd, the Beelzebub of my homosexuality. He said that I should get rid of Floyd or concede that analysis to cure my homosexuality had failed, and although he would continue to see me, I should stop kidding myself.

One other thing. I thought Aschenbach's love for Tadzio was transcendent, a man in love with beauty itself, but I forgot that in the end Aschenbach dies because of it.

Johnny Minotaur

On June 9th, 1971, Bob Feiden gave me two tickets to a midnight screening of a surrealist movie by Charles Henri Ford called *Johnny Minotaur*. The invitation included a party afterward, and I asked Floyd to come along with me. Charles Henri Ford was a loopy, drug-addicted homosexual with a small family inheritance who led a happily debauched life. He had been part of Gertrude Stein's salon of friends, a sometimes court jester to Somerset Maugham, and the one-time editor of *View*, a magazine about surrealism. Ford lived at the Dakota on West 72nd Street, and spent many summers on a Greek island, photographing the good times with a 16 mm handheld camera. That midnight screening was the debut of his magnum opus, narrated by Allen Ginsberg and Salvador Dalí, incomprehensibly, as it would turn out.

The Bleecker Street theater was overflowing with night crawlers, hipsters, underground celebrities, and leather boys. It was so crowded that Prince Egon von Fürstenberg had to sit on the floor with Jonas Mekas. Wandering up and down the aisle was a deeply tanned woman who was searching for a friend in the audience. She was wearing hot pants, a lamentable fashion trend of the moment, and a halter top with no bra, which made her voluptuous breasts look like *karpouzi* in a mesh bag, her dark nipples visible through the tan fabric. Her hair was hooker-style, piled high on her head, tendrils hanging down around her face, like a trannie on Tenth Avenue. Another freaky sideshow character at a midnight screening in the Village.

Floyd felt different. "Wow, nice tits," Floyd said, exhaling a sigh of desire. He had the worst taste in women.

"I bet she's a man," I told him. "Or started out as one."

The woman finally spotted her friend, a geeky bald guy in a jean jacket with bottle-thick John Lennon eyeglasses. He had buttons with sayings pinned all over his jean jacket, including one that said, *You suck my soul and I'll blow your mind.*

Floyd was still staring at her as the lights dimmed and the movie flickered to a start. It was a grainy home movie, overexposed and washed out. I spent forty-five minutes trying to figure out if I was watching highbrow art that I was too callow to understand, or if all that mattered was that I was bored. Anyway, the highly anticipated scene, in which an adolescent cut a hole in a warm melon that had been baking in the Mediterranean sun, and fucked the hole with a pale, uncircumcised penis that looked like a white asparagus, wasn't erotic, or funny, and wasn't art. The movie ended abruptly mid-scene, the film intentionally torn at the end so the theater was blasted by the blinding white light of a blank screen, to wake up the viewer, assumedly. The Bleecker Street audience burst into enthusiastic applause.

As people began to make their way up the center aisle toward the exit, Floyd pushed past me and positioned himself next to the exaggerated woman with the large breasts. Up close she was a little tired around the edges, older than she had looked across the theater. She smiled, and for a moment I saw someone else living under that wig and makeup, but she had no clue who it was. Why that crazy getup? I wondered. Floyd flashed her a Super Sexy Floyd grin, like a horny cartoon puppy randy for a roll in the rye.

The woman smiled back politely. We introduced ourselves. Her name was Phyllis Weintraub. A Jewish girl. "What did you think of the movie?" she asked Floyd as we slowly moved up the aisle.

"That melon scene was *too much*," was Floyd's critical assessment, followed by another goofy dog grin.

"What did *you* think of the movie?" she asked me, with a coy smile, as if we were sharing some inside joke. I thought for a second maybe the joke was Floyd.

"The movie was the pits," I said. "And the pits didn't come from the melon."

I'm not exactly sure what this meant, but Ms. Weintraub and her odd friend got a good laugh out of it.

We slowed to a halt under the bright lights of the Bleecker Street marquee while Floyd and Phyllis eyed each other. Floyd was emanating I-need-to-get-laid pheromones and Ms. Weintraub was eyeing his tennis player thighs in his turned-up jean shorts. "I could go for a cappuccino," Ms. Weintraub said.

"Not me," I piped in.

"I'll go," Floyd said eagerly.

That traitor.

"Catch you later, Glen!" Floyd said, trying to mollify me with "Glen."

"I guess we both got dumped," said Ms. Weintraub's spooky friend.

I looked at him like I didn't know what he was talking about. He had very stoned eyes behind his John Lennon glasses.

"Do you want to get a cup of java with me?" he asked. "Or are you going to the party?"

"To the party," I said, taking one last glance at Floyd and Ms. Weintraub hailing a taxi.

I was exasperated, in the kind of emotional turmoil a three-year-old might experience in having his favorite toy taken away. I walked off in the direction of the Bowery, my head buried between my shoulders. I half listened to the person chattering next to me as we walked through the Village. His name was Bob, he said he produced a documentary called *Groupies* that was being released that summer, and he was the casting agent of a new film in production called *The French Connection*. From the pocket of his button-festooned jean jacket, he produced a badly wrapped joint in sweet-tasting colored rolling paper. We passed it between us in the street on the way to the party. "Why was your friend dressed like that?" I asked him.

"Phyllis? Like what?"

"You know, big hair, hot pants . . ."

We walked in silence as he thought about this. "She's overcompensating. She was sick," he said, exhaling marijuana smoke into the air.

"Sick?"

"She had cancer," he said. "Hodgkin's. She beat it, though."

"I'm sorry to hear your friend was sick." I wondered if she told Floyd, or if it even mattered.

"What do you do?" he asked.

"I move furniture in an auction gallery," I said.

I thought that would shut him up, but instead he said, "From where to where?"

"From people's houses or apartments or sometimes just up and down the aisle at the auctions," I said. He shook his head and scrunched up his face like he'd tasted something sour, so I added, "I went to film school."

"A lot of good that did you," he said.

I didn't say anything the rest of the way to the grimy loft building on Great Jones Street, where the party was being held. We rode up together in a delivery elevator to the fifth floor, where the metal door opened on a huge canvas of mayhem and blasting music, candles everywhere, an invitation to an inferno.

"Have a good night," I told the man, effectively ditching him. I didn't mean to be rude, but I guess he was insulted.

"Well, fuck you," he said petulantly, and walked off into the crowd.

The party was packed, and I had to thread my way to the bar. Although it was June there were red Christmas tree lights and red votive candles on the tables and windowsills. Warhol superstar Jackie Curtis was there, dripping with glitter, and the tall, delicate, bleached-blond Candy Darling, who puffed on a rhinestone cigarette holder, seemed to have captured the complete attention of socialite Pat Buckley, the wife of William F. Buckley, who sat next to her on a windowsill. Jim Morrison was passed out on the floor in a corner. Warhol superstar, Edie Sedgwick, was locked in the bathroom performing cunnilingus on a woman she had just met. Paul Morrissey, arrived along with Lady St Just and a very tipsy Tennessee Williams in tow.

I can repeat all these details not because I remember them, but only because the writer Dotson Rader was at this extraordinary gathering, and he wrote about it many years later in his memoir about his friendship with Tennessee Williams called *Cry of the Heart*. I remember very little of the details because someone handed me yet another joint, this one probably had Angel Dust in it, and I was extraterrestrial. What I do remember was that a man in leather pants put handcuffs on me and led me stumbling around the room, and then he took a fire extinguisher off the wall and sprayed everyone with it. He and I were thrown out of the party, and I rode down in the elevator with him. Out on the street I asked him to un-cuff me.

He asked, "Are you positive you want to go free?"

I said, yes, I was positive, and he un-cuffed me on Wooster Street and I walked home.

Floyd called the next day to say that he was going to Saltaire, a small family community on Fire Island, with Phyllis Weintraub, and that he would be back Monday. If any of his drug dealer friends called, I should say he was out of town on business. I was spitting angry that he was deserting me for the big-busted harlot, and I couldn't think of enough things negative to say about her. I spent the rest of the weekend frothing at the mouth, so distracted at the auction gallery sale on Saturday that I dropped a fake Chinese import lamp on the floor and shattered it. Ziggy filed an insurance claim for $1,700.

I didn't hear from Floyd until Monday afternoon. "I think I'm in love," he said goofily.

"You're out of your fucking mind," I said.

Floyd said he was so smitten with Phyllis that he might even break up with Ellyn. He said she had the sweetest pussy he had ever tasted and that sex with her was fan-tas-tic, man, despite the fact she was an ancient thirty-two years old, twelve years older than he, a deplorable age difference, I told him.

"Do you know who Phyllis *is*?" he asked excitedly. "She's the girlfriend of—" He mentioned the name of a famous, and married, rock and roll manager from Los Angeles. Floyd said he was going to spend the whole summer with Ms. Weintraub in Saltaire, and asked if I wanted to visit them. Visit them! I wanted to napalm them. I harrumphed that having sex with an old woman in exchange for a summer on Fire Island was sleazy, and that he was nothing more than a prostitute, and I would certainly not be visiting. My voice broke when I told him that my summer was ruined without him around, and the least he could do was come to the city to visit me once in a while. Pathetic.

"She has *cancer*," I whispered hoarsely.

"Who told you that?" he asked.

"Her weird friend from the movie theater. Who knows what you can get from fucking her."

"You can't get cancer fucking," he said, and hung up on me, one of the few good choices he ever made.

He was gone. I was cored, eviscerated. The thought of never seeing him again sucked the breath right out of me. Floyd. Jesus. Was this feeling of desperation love? I couldn't understand what I was feeling, subsumed by longing and sorrow, and then rigid with anxiety. You could see it in my face and in my posture. I became so anxious that I couldn't swallow food. Everything tasted awful, even Chinese food.

Then one day it hit me. It was exactly the sensation I had if I didn't bend to all the compulsive behavior of my childhood—unrelenting anxiety so monstrously fierce, it literally took my breath away. I had OCD about a person. But there was no magic ritual to undo the compulsion of Floyd. Touching things twice or counting to twenty would not sate the hunger for Floyd. That summer I slept and sweated and smoked cigarettes and joints. I drank red wine during the day, went to work at the gallery on Saturday mornings drunk. I remembered how Floyd had to arrange his cock at an angle to fit into his jockey shorts. I withered away in the stinking Manhattan summer, holed up in my basement bedroom. Feverishly, I watched despair and desire dance a *pas de deux* at the foot of my bed like little monsters.

There were no cell phones then. The beach shack Floyd was staying in had no phone. If he wanted to call me, there was only a pay phone at the dock. But of course, he didn't want to call me. He lolled on the beach every day at Saltaire, deeply tanned, his Afghan hair streaked from the sun, fucking the floozie in the late afternoons on clean white sheets, eating her pussy while white-tail deer grazed behind their isolated beach shack. I knew this because I saw it in my fevered dreams, in my nighttime dreams and my daytime dreams, in my erotic reveries, until I couldn't take a breath without breathing Floyd.

"Are you okay?" the people who ran the auction gallery asked one day, when I was nearly catatonic trying to glue a leg onto a Chippendale reproduction but couldn't quite fit the pieces together. Even as I was reassuring them I was okay, tears ran down my cheeks. "Oh, you're just in love, you'll get over it," the owner's wife said, mortifying me that everybody knew I was so in love with Floyd.

Dr. Myers enthused that Floyd's departure was good riddance. He said I should seize the opportunity to break from Floyd, to make new friends with young professionals who didn't use drugs, and I should find a job with a future. I needed to do physical exercise to combat the anxiety, and most of all, I should stop going to Max's Kansas City. But the last thing I could give up that summer was my Max's Mad Hatter's psilocybin tea party.

Finally, it was September. The season on Fire Island was over, the house in Saltaire was being closed up, and Phyllis's usefulness to Floyd was ending. So he dumped her. I couldn't believe what I was hearing on the phone. They "weren't a match," Floyd decided, that moron, and I happily agreed with him that they weren't a match. I was a moron, too. I invited him to bunk with me again and let him use my apartment as a base for dealing drugs. The day after Labor Day he moved back in. My grandmother used to say, "Celebrate poor man, shit is cheap."

Floyd and I fell back into the same routine, until one day he produced two plane tickets to Puerto Rico. He said he was given the use of someone's apartment in Old San Juan for a week, and he asked me if I wanted to go with him. I was thrilled to have Floyd to myself for a week in Puerto Rico, until I looked at the plane tickets and discovered someone else's name was on it. I asked Floyd why there were fake names on the tickets, and demanded to know if he was going to be smuggling drugs and he swore he wasn't. The names on the tickets were simply the names of the people who gave him the tickets instead of paying him for drugs. We got into an argument about how dangerous it was to use the tickets and the next day Floyd left for the airport without me. He was arrested at the check-in for using a ticket purchased with a stolen credit card, and when the police searched his luggage, they found 500 Tuinals in a plastic bag.

Late that night I went to a Brooklyn courthouse and bailed him out with money I'd borrowed from my grandmother. It was after midnight by the time he was released, and I was waiting for him at the side door of the jail when a woman pulled up to the curb in a navy blue convertible BMW with the top down and the radio blasting Diana Ross singing, "Ain't No Mountain High Enough." I had never met Ellyn, but I recognized her cleavage from the topless photos Floyd had shown me. The courthouse door opened and Floyd emerged, his eyes clear and greener than ever. He gave me a sweet smile and hugged me tight, towering over me, rocking us from side to side while he embraced me. "Thanks, Glen," he whispered in my hair. Then he got behind the steering wheel of Ellyn's car and drove off with her in the passenger seat. He never looked back. I watched them turn toward the Brooklyn Bridge to Manhattan as she leaned over from the passenger seat and her head disappeared onto his lap.

Going home, I stared at my reflection in a subway car window. It was like the end of the movie *Sunday Bloody Sunday*, when the wonderful British actor Peter Finch breaks the fourth wall and talks into the camera. Finch plays a middle-aged Jewish doctor in London, and he and Glenda Jackson, a divorcee with a humdrum job, are in love with the same young guy, a bisexual sculptor played by Murray Head. At the end of the movie the younger man deserts them both and goes off to America without a care. In the closing moments Finch, his beautiful blue eyes filled with tears, looks into the camera and says, "They say, 'What's half a loaf? You're well shot of him.' I know that, but I miss him, that's all. They say, 'He never made you happy,' and I say, I am happy, apart from missing him . . . All my life I've been looking for somebody courageous, resourceful. He's not it. But *something*."

Maybe that's all gay men get, only something. Floyd was something.

Beaten up and bleeding, I stumbled through the world that broiling summer, burning the days, worshipping nights at Max's, not being with men, not being with women, swallowed up by self-pity in a city that loves to swallow sad people and spit them out. No better place in the world to be depressed. The city was black and gray that autumn, there were no pretty leaves. It got dark early, and by mid-November it was icy cold out. Oddly, I never felt so much a part of the city as I did that winter. I was a piece of the gritty puzzle of Manhattan. I was one of its nine million stories, whatever my story would turn out to be. If only it would turn out to be something.

Phyllis Weintraub Redux

The following spring, after I watched Floyd drive into the night with his girlfriend, a woman stopped in the street in front of my townhouse and peered into the window.

I've replayed this scene thousands of times in my head, and I've seen too many Nora Ephron movies to know which parts I've embellished. What I remember for certain is that Neil Young's *After the Gold Rush* album was on the KLH, on automatic repeat, and that I played it and played it until the music and lyrics had been imprinted in my mind and it had become the de facto soundtrack of my being. I also know that the sun was so bright, it ricocheted off the windows of St. Vincent's Hospital across the street, filling my apartment with the kind of intense yellow sunlight you only see simulated in stage productions. And I remember that at first I didn't recognize the neat and attractive woman in a business suit.

She had big brown Semitic eyes, and her hair was chestnut colored and straight. She was carrying a leather portfolio under her arm. I stared back at her, and when she smiled at me, I went to the window and opened it, letting in the crisp spring air.

"I was on my way home," she said hesitantly. "I live on Morton Street and I was walking down Eleventh Street and I saw you through the window. I thought I'd take the opportunity to say 'no hard feelings.'"

I crouched down to see her better. My God, it was Phyllis Weintraub, that louse who took Floyd to Fire Island last summer. But how can this elegant woman be the same hooker travesty I met at the Bleecker Street Cinema?

"I know you hate me," she said. "Floyd told me you did. But truth is, I did you a favor."

"I don't hate you," I said. "At least not anymore. I just didn't recognize you at first. You look so different."

She squinted, the sun in her eyes, and something crossed her mind that she quickly dismissed from saying. "There have been a lot of changes," she answered finally.

"I can tell. You look great."

"Do you see Floyd anymore?" she asked.

"Not since I bailed him out of jail."

We both laughed at this, then she looked down the street and back at me. Her hair was three different colors of brown. She was beautiful.

"Well, it was nice to see you," she said.

"Yes. Thanks for stopping to say hello."

Suddenly, I had an odd, yet familiar prickly feeling in my chest.

"Yes. Take care," she said.

"You too," I choked. I could hardly speak.

"You too."

She turned and walked down the street, and I stuck my head out the window to watch her. She got about six houses away before I realized what that awful tight feeling in my chest was; if I let her get away, nothing would ever calm me. For a moment I was frightened. So before I could think, I raced out the front door of my house and into the street, calling after her, "Wait! Wait!"

She stopped and turned. When I caught up to her, out of breath, I gasped, "Do you have time to come in for a cup of coffee?"

"You have no shoes on," she said.

We went back to the apartment, where I was a nervous wreck. I tried to make coffee, but it turned out I didn't have any, and there was only one tea bag, which had been in a drawer for a year. But what I did have was a chilled bottle of Pouilly-Fuissé in the refrigerator, and although it was kind of early in the day to drink wine, we said what the hell.

"That night I met you at the movie theater?" I asked, sitting at the dining room table. "It was like you were in a disguise."

"Floyd said you told him I was a hooker," she said.

Oh shit, God knows what else Floyd told her. "I'm so sorry."

"No, don't apologize," she said. "It was the best compliment I heard in a long while—that I looked good enough to be paid."

I smiled and we toasted to looking good enough to be paid.

"I had been sick," she said.

"Floyd told me. I'm sorry."

"That night was my first time out in a long time," she said. "All my hair had fallen out in patches, so I was wearing that ridiculous wig."

"It was eye-catching," I said.

"I was overcompensating, and you sort of lose judgment."

I asked how she was doing now. She said she'd been in remission for nearly six months. She knocked wood on the table.

"I feel really badly for all the mean things I said about you to Floyd," I admitted, looking down at the table in embarrassment.

"Oh, don't beat yourself up. You were hurting. You were in love."

Hearing her say that made me wince. "I *wasn't* in love," I said.

"Oh, okay," she agreed, not very convincingly.

I asked what was in the portfolio she was carrying and it turned out she was a union stylist who worked mainly in TV commercials. It was stuffed with drawings of men dressed as the fruit in the Fruit of the Loom underwear logo, a project she was working on. She had spent all day searching for the right leotards that would stick out under the costumes. She was curious about how I came to work at the auction gallery, and I told her how we tagged up the entire contents of a man's life and sold it on the lawn of his house one Saturday morning, and that a hundred people walked away with pieces of him. We talked for a long time, until late in the afternoon, all talked out, we quieted down and listened to the music playing on the stereo. Neil Young was singing "After the Gold Rush," and I began to sing along with his sweet, reedy falsetto.

Phyllis laughed at my imitation of Neil Young.

Nobody knows what those lyrics mean, not even Neil Young himself, he claims. It's their ambiguity that makes them mystical for so many people. Particularly for stoners. My bedroom was in the basement level of the townhouse, and I was waiting down there for replacements, for backup, for help, and now the sun had burst through the sky, and perhaps that light was Phyllis. I was thinking about what a friend had said, that I would never be straight and I should stop kidding myself, and I was hoping it was a lie, and this woman would belie it with me.

It turned out that Neil Young was appearing at Carnegie Hall the following week, so we made a date for a week from Friday, and I walked her out to the front stoop, and watched as she walked down the block, and all the anxiety was gone, like I had touched something twice.

Neither of us wanted it to seem like it was a real date, so we met on Sheridan Square, about halfway between where we lived, and took the subway uptown. For some reason all my suave was gone and I was nervous and chatty. After the beautiful and moving Neil Young concert, we went back to the village and got rare burgers and beer at Chumley's, an old Greenwich Village speakeasy and pub hidden down a pretty courtyard. We talked about Philadelphia, where she grew up, and that she wanted to be in the fashion business, which was why she left home when she was nineteen. She came to New York to work in the fashion industry, where she met her ex-husband, a successful clothing manufacturer. When they divorced, she insisted on giving him back the jewelry he'd bought her, even her diamond wedding ring. She wanted a clean break, no hard feelings, although he was cheating on her. She dated a lot of wealthy men, including Barbara Walters's ex-husband, and the president of a Fifth Avenue jewelers, but she wasn't interested in money anymore, she wanted to be in love. Around midnight I walked with her to the apartment building she lived in on Morton Street.

I kissed her in the elevator, and we necked in the hallway outside her door like furtive teenagers, until it became something more, and we needed to go inside. Her apartment was feminine, the bedroom was pink, and she was demure in bed, at first. Later, she said, "If you're wondering, you're much better." She meant Floyd. Of course, it crossed my mind once or twice or maybe a dozen times while we were *in flagrante* about how I compared with Floyd in the sack, and intuitively, she brought it up.

"But he's bigger," I said. An incredibly dumb response.

"That's not the way it felt," she responded. An incredibly smart response. I shut up.

Yes, her body was older-looking—she was, after all, eight years older than me, which seemed like a lot to a callow twenty-four-year-old. The next morning when we got up, I realized there were purple felt pens all over her apartment, on every table, and when I asked her why, she said, "I like purple."

"But that's *terrible*," I wailed, and somehow, with that proprietary exclamation, we were involved.

The last person to whom I thought I'd have to defend Phyllis was Dr. Myers. I expected he'd be thrilled, but instead he seemed disturbed when I told him we were having an affair. "Isn't this the same woman that your friend Floyd had a sexual relationship with?" he asked. I said she was. "Do you ever think that his penis was inside her and that's part of why you have intercourse with her?" he asked. I lied and said no. However, I did think that, and it was a turn-on. He asked about what we did in bed; did I have vaginal sex with her from behind? Because if we did it doggie style, that would mean I was having homosexual sex with her. "Does this bring to mind the basic Oedipal scene?" he asked. "Where you put your penis where your father's had been?"

He was so annoying. "Why does it have to be about my mother and father?" I asked.

"Because Phyllis is a mother figure," he said. "This is your real triumph over your father, sleeping with Phyllis, who is subconsciously your mother."

That's when I yelled at him for the first time in nearly ten years. "*Why do you have to ruin this by comparing it to sleeping with my mother?*" I shouted. "*Why can't you just let me enjoy this, whatever it is? Isn't this what you wanted?*"

"Why does it make you angry if I suggest you've chosen a mother figure to have relations with?" He was indefatigable.

"*Oh come on!*" I said. "*I did not choose a mother figure!*" I catapulted up from the couch. "She chose *me*. She saw something in me and she chose me." Then I walked out. I had never walked out on a session. I swore I would never return. But of course, I did.

I don't remember the interstitial material that made the relationship a romance. It's like a shuttlecock weaving in a loom. The incremental sharing of experience slowly assembled itself into our private world. The rest is ephemera. There was no special moment that heralded the advent of love that I can tell you about. I still don't know what love is. I know that we were kind to each other, selflessly, and I was deliriously dedicated to her momentary happiness. She was fun, smart, great to be with. What's more, she seemed to delight in me. I made her happy. I remember that I could not wait to be with her when we were apart, and no minutia of her life was too small to entrance me. "Did you have to wait very long for the train this morning?" I asked. Or, "I know I just called you five minutes ago, but what was the name of that good dry cleaners on Hudson Street?" Or, "If I can get out of the gallery early today, do you want to see a six o'clock movie at the Paris Theater?" The kitchen was rearranged so a person could actually cook, and there was food in the refrigerator, which had previously been an empty white space with a moldy jam ring on the second shelf. We had cheese and eggs and salad dressing. She also irritated me. She was always in the bathroom when I wanted to use it, and I didn't want that shirt laundered, I wanted it dry-cleaned, and I did not want to hike to Gristedes at midnight to get milk when the Korean grocery was just across Greenwich Avenue. But I did. That's the tell.

Were we in love? Or were we in some bad Tennessee Williams play? Was this a B movie? Why would she choose to be with a gay man and why would I chose to be with an older, sick woman? Was there some unspoken pact, that she gave me a shot at a heterosexual life? Or was I able to love her *because* of her illness and our relationship would be finite? It certainly wasn't *Tea and Sympathy*, that wonderful movie I saw at the Culver Theater starring Deborah Kerr as the middle-aged wife of a tough headmaster of a military school, a bully with a secret. Kerr takes a sensitive, tormented seventeen-year-old student, who is suspected of being a "sister-boy," to bed with her to prove to him that he's not homosexual, and to satisfy her own desires. Before she has sex with him, Kerr says to the boy, "Years from now, when you talk about this—and you will—be kind."

Sometimes lying in bed, Phyllis would say that line to me and we would laugh. And sometimes I said it to her and it was just as funny the other way around.

One night we were strolling around the West Village, looking in the windows of townhouses, and I told Phyllis about how when I was a young kid in Brooklyn I used to take long bus trips on the 18th Avenue bus to the end of the line and back, looking in the windows of houses and apartment buildings, wondering who I would have been if I lived there, or there.

"And now you know who you are," she said.

"Do I?" I wondered. "At least now I know which house I live in."

Interstitial

I stopped going to Max's Kansas City, and my assortment of *rara avis* friends molted away. I became a part of Phyllis's crowd, older married couples with kids in middle school. Strangely, even though I had no interest in the tribulations of parenthood, I enjoyed being part of Phyllis's crowd. At first her friends were dubious about me. Some of them had met Floyd during Phyllis's summer dalliance; now Phyllis was dating his once-jealous boyfriend. What was that about? But the most cynical of her close friends soon saw how loving we were, that we clearly cared about each other, and they embraced her happiness, if not mine.

I went to Brooklyn one night and told my mother and father that I was having an affair with an older woman, who had moved in with me, and that I thought I was in love. They listened with the wary smiles of passengers on the deck of the *Titanic* trying to enjoy the band. My parents, once staunch supporters of my dreams and endeavors, anxious for me to find peace, had in recent years become more cautious about my undertakings. I was living in a Manhattan townhouse with no money. Now I was in love with an older woman. "How much older?" my mother asked, shuddering to think. I told them the truth; she was eight years older.

They exchanged glances across the table. At least she wasn't eighty-two.

"There's something else," I said. "She was sick, but she's okay now."

"Sick? How?" my father asked.

I told them she had Hodgkin's but she was in remission.

Yup, the *Titanic*. I could see it in their faces.

They managed to say they were happy for me, and asked to meet her. I suggested that Phyllis be my date at my cousin Marilyn's wedding at a catering hall in Flatbush in a few weeks. When I got home and told Phyllis, she was terrified. I'd never seen her so nervous as she was about meeting them. I promised her that as long as she didn't have two heads, they would be delighted with her, but I could tell by the way she fretted over what to wear (she was a stylist for a living, she told other people what to wear) that she was nervous. She wore, as best I can remember, a black dress and a white silk shawl, and she looked classy and made me proud.

The big day came, we walked into the garish catering hall in Brooklyn with red flocked wallpaper and rows of fake crystal chandeliers, and I spotted my mom and dad on a mezzanine up three steps where there was a crowd of people near the smorgasbord table. They waved, Phyllis and I smiled at each other and took a deep breath, and we headed toward them, grinning like fools. Phyllis was so nervous, she misjudged the height of the first step up to the mezzanine, and she pitched forward and fell on her knees *up* the two steps, breaking her fall with her hands and ripping the back seam of her dress. I felt so bad for Phyllis; my heart broke. My father and I dove forward to pick her up, and as we helped her to her feet, she smiled and said, "Well, you can't say I don't make an entrance."

My parents were terrific. They didn't miss a beat. It was a kosher catering hall and my dad made a joke about hiring a kosher lawyer to sue over the steps. He was sort of goofy around Phyllis, and on his best behavior. I'd never seen him like that before. I think he kind of fancied her. He went to get her a soft drink from the bar, and my mother got a needle and

thread from the front office and took Phyllis into one of the
bridesmaid's dressing rooms where she stitched up the tear in
her dress. By the time they returned, they were best friends.
When I looked across the dance floor, I saw my mother and
Phyllis sitting at a table, talking. I got misty watching them,
thinking that this was what we all wanted, what we all worked
toward. It was happening and it was good. It dawned on me
that perhaps Phyllis and my mother were talking about *me*,
and I didn't want Phyllis to be in cahoots with my mom, so
I rushed to the table reeking of insecurity, and blurted out,
"You're not talking about me, are you?"

They stared at me, amazed. "No," my mother said. "We
were talking about shopping at Loehmann's."

"Oh," I said, disappointed.

The smorgasbord had chopped liver swans and ice sculp-
tures. Later at dinner we sat with distant relatives, one of
whom immediately inquired about the nature of our relationship. Phyllis took the lead and said, "We're friends." After
dinner the band played and Phyllis encouraged me to ask my
mother to dance, and my father asked Phyllis to dance. We
were all beaming at each other fox-trotting around the dance
floor. It was corny but I will never forget it.

The next night I spoke to my mom on the phone and she
told me how much she liked Phyllis. "Are you in this for the
duration?" she asked. I told her I didn't know what the "duration" was.

She paused and said, "Try to make this last."

A time went by. I can't say if it was a long time or short.
Until one sleepy Sunday morning in bed in my bedroom, listening to the calming hiss of the radiator letting off steam, I
rolled over to face Phyllis and found her lying on her back,
staring at the ceiling.

"What's the matter, Phyll?" I asked.

She shook her head a little and I searched for her hand under the covers. She took my hand in hers and slowly raised it to her neck. She put my fingers on a spot just above her left collarbone where there was a small bump. I pulled my hand away like I had gotten a shock, but I was terrified that I was feeling death.

"It's back," she said, sounding pissed off. She turned her head toward me on the pillow.

"You don't know that," I said. "That bump could be anything. It could be an insect bite."

"I know what it is," she said, and I knew not to challenge her.

The following morning, we went to her internists' office at Memorial Hospital, and he discovered nodes in her groin as well. I could see the dismay on the doctor's face that it was back so soon. Recurrent. Metastasized? He couldn't be sure until the tests came back, but we knew. For the next two days we robotically pretended we were going on with our lives, but our lives had stopped and we were blind and breathless. I wasn't even in the apartment when the doctor called and said it was stage IV, and they were going to treat it aggressively. When I came home from the auction gallery Phyllis said almost off-handedly, "I would understand if you choose to run."

"Run? Are you crazy? Why would I run?" We both sobbed like babies, hugging tightly. I told her over and over that she would beat it back, beat it back. When we finally calmed down, as an act of defiance we ordered a good bottle of wine delivered from the liquor store and Chinese food. We ate shrimp and lobster sauce, and I tried to make conversation, but no matter what I said to distract us, it sounded trivial and false.

I called my mother the next day and told her. She asked me what I was going to do and I said, "The duration." I told my mother that I was afraid I didn't have the mettle to help

Phyllis die. My mother said that often a crisis like this brings out the best in people, and she believed I had it in me to help Phyllis through. I tried my best, but I was an amateur at death and dying. I sometimes would excuse myself and go into the bathroom and quietly bang my head against the wall. The chemo was punishing. Her hair fell out for the second time and she shed weight overnight. We pretended her figure was better than ever. But it wasn't the figure of a thin woman, it was the figure of a sick person, and her eyes were sunken. When the chemotherapy ended, she was so pale that her skin was translucent.

Her friends and family insisted we go to Miami Beach for a few weeks so she could recover in the sun, and somebody bought us plane tickets and loaned us a condo, and even paid for a rental car. She was nearly lifeless the whole time we were down there. I never saw anybody barely alive struggling for another day, another hour, but she somehow fought her way to a chaise lounge by the pool every day and lay motionless in the sun, a big hat covering her bald head.

"I made a decision," she said one day from beneath the hat. "I'm going to ignore this thing."

I said I thought that was a good idea, and we shook hands on it. We told each other that with the chemo over, we had closed a bad chapter in our lives and we were moving on.

The night we got back from Miami, she was so exhausted from traveling that I had to carry her down the narrow staircase to the bedroom. I'll never forget how light she was, her arms around my neck, eyes wide like a frightened child. I put her into bed and she drifted off to sleep even as I pulled the covers over her, so I doubt she heard me whisper, "I have to find a parking spot for the car."

Since it was going to be a tough job to find a legal space for the Volkswagen Bug I was driving, and since Phyllis was already asleep, and since it wasn't even midnight and Max's was just getting started, it wouldn't make any difference if I spent an hour looking for a legal space, or if I dropped in at my old haunt.

Marjoe

I slipped into the back room of Max's like a hand into a well-worn leather glove. All of my cronies were there in the red light, the high, the low, the princes and princesses. There was a seat available on the banquette along the back wall, right next to my favorite, Bob Feiden.

"Greetings to you, my Mister Gaines," he began. "Are you visiting us tonight from the straight world? Are you in a split level in Levittown yet?"

I told him to stop being mean, that Phyllis wasn't well again, and I had just hours ago arrived back from Miami, where we went so she could recuperate from her recent round of chemo.

"I'm so sorry," he said. "I didn't know." He said that he was always fond of Phyllis and that he would hope for the best.

When I told him I was taking care of her, and she was asleep in my bed, he looked disturbed. "That's an enormous task, taking care of someone," he said.

I nodded and looked around the room at all the characters and antics I had left behind and I was afraid I'd start to cry again. Feiden saw this and said, "You must allow your friends to cheer you up!" He made room for me on the banquette and waved down a waitress. He ordered a bottle of Pouilly for me, and for himself a *greps* tonic.

"You must stay for a while and meet this man named 'Marjoe,'" Feiden insisted. This was the latest Person of Interest who had appeared on his radar. Feiden explained that

Howard Smith, the columnist and publisher of the *Village Voice*, and the writer Sarah Kernochan, had raised $300,000 to produce and direct a feature documentary about a man who was a Pentecostal child evangelist.

Sure enough when Marjoe arrived, he certainly was imposing. He was a strapping man in his late twenties with a head of peroxided curls and a practiced smile. He wore turquoise jewelry and $1,000 alligator cowboy boots. Marjoe's date that night was with Berry Berenson, the granddaughter of designer Elsa Schiaparelli, who was obviously very taken with him. The Pentecostals say they speak in tongues, and whatever Marjoe uttered that night held everyone at the table spellbound. The name "Marjoe" was a combination of Mary and Joseph, and it was given to him as part of a promotional scheme by his parents, who had been Pentecostal evangelists on the tent circuit in the 1930s. He was ordained when he was four years old, and in a wartime publicity stunt, Marjoe married a sailor on a weekend pass to his girlfriend in Long Beach, California. A photo of the tiny preacher marrying the couple, with his permed curls and made-to-order tiny cowboy boots embossed with gold crucifixes on the sides, a Bible in his hands, a fist raised to the heavens, was published across the country. *Marjoe the Miracle Child* became a headliner on the Pentecostal tent circuit, performing melodramatic fake healings and selling "miracle handkerchiefs" for $5 each.

For a little kid he was one hell of a preacher, too. In his pipsqueaky voice he would pound the small podium his parents built for him and demand of the congregants, "Can God deliver an al-co-hol-ic? *Yes he can!* Can God deliver a homo-sexual? *Yes he can!*" The real miracle was that a child was able to memorize complex sermons, but Marjoe's mom had a method to get the boy's attention. She waterboarded her child. When his attention strayed, she would hold his head under water in the sink. Marjoe became a star on the evangelical circuit, and by the time he'd reached his early teens, he claimed to have earned millions of dollars—all of which his father absconded with, he claimed.

After his voice changed, he spent a dozen years in the secular world drifting from job to job, and he had recently gone back to "preaching the blood." His fevered sermons were delivered with left hand on his hip, the microphone held high, prancing up and down the aisles like Mick Jagger, preaching on the blood like Elmer Gantry. He was a showman of the first order, and a gifted preacher. And a fake. And he was going to expose it all in the documentary they were making about him.

"You should write a book," I enthused that night in Max's.

"Practically everybody I met in my entire life said I should write a book," Marjoe said. "But where do you find a writer?"

Feiden started to say something—he knew plenty of writers—when I interrupted. "I'm a writer," I lied. "Can I write your book?"

I looked at Feiden, who was fuming.

Marjoe never inquired what I'd written, or if I could write. It happened that simply, off the cuff. He said, "If you can sell it to a publisher, you can write it."

We agreed we'd go 50-50, shook hands, and exchanged phone numbers.

Feiden was beyond furious. When Marjoe left the table, he said he would never introduce me to anyone again.

"What did I do?" I asked.

"You're a liar and an opportunist," he said.

"I am not!" I said, standing to leave. An opportunity had just presented itself and I grabbed it. That's what I was waiting for, right?

"What are you going to do?" he asked.

"I'm going to write his book."

"Highly doubtful. Good luck to you," Feiden said, and I got up and left.

I just knew that Feiden was going to call Marjoe the next day and expose me as a furniture mover in a crap gallery. I drove back to my apartment in tears, and as a sign from the muse, I found a parking spot just down the block from the townhouse. Phyllis was still sound asleep, just as I had left her. I got out my aqua blue Smith Corona Coronet portable electric typewriter, put it on the dining room table, smoked a joint, and wrote, with the fearless confidence of the ignorant, a book proposal. The purple prose poured out of my head. I didn't even think about it: "*There are hundreds of them out there every night*," the proposal began breathlessly. "*They come from the flat plains of the Midwest and the big cities of the East. They come to see Marjoe, the Miracle Child, anointed by God . . .*" It went on like that for nine more pages.

The next morning when Phyllis woke up, she was groggy and I brought her tea in bed. I sat next to her with the nine pages in my hand and excitedly told her about the night before, about not being able to find a space and ducking into Max's.

"You went to Max's?" she asked. We both knew what Max's meant. "I thought you had outgrown Max's."

"Yes, yes," I said. "You were asleep and I couldn't find a parking space so I ducked in for a drink, no big deal." It sounded like so much bullshit. The truth was I was upset and tired and scared, and needed to dip my toes outside the netherworld of my home.

"It's okay that you went to Max's," she said unconvincingly.

"Listen, Phyll, I'm sorry I went to Max's, but it wasn't to get into trouble. Bottom line, I ran into Bob Feiden—he always knows the next big thing—and he introduced me to this guy, Marjoe. It's a combination of Mary and Joseph. They're making a documentary about him. He was a child preacher. His parents were Pentecostal evangelists and they ordained him at age six. They're making a documentary about him, and he's going to expose all the Pentecostal evangelists. All the fake healing and rolling around on the floor. And I'm going to write his biography."

She shook her head as she tried to process what she had just heard. "Why would you be writing his book?"

"I asked him if I could write it and he said yes."

"You asked him to write his biography and he said yes? Just like that?"

"Yes!" I said.

"Did he ask you for money?"

"No, no. You have the wrong idea."

"And you wrote a book proposal overnight?"

"Just listen. Just listen."

Phyllis settled back on the pillows, holding her cup of tea between the palms of her hands.

"*There are hundreds of them out there every night*," I intoned solemnly, as if God were saying, "Let there be light!" "*They come from the flat plains of the Midwest and the big cities of the East. They come to see Marjoe, the Miracle Child, anointed by God . . .*"

She listened quietly to the rest of it, her expression changing as she became more interested in the story. "And you wrote all this last night?" she asked when I was finished.

"I swear."

"You had a busy night while I was sleeping."

"Don't be angry that I went to Max's." Then I thought, what a thoughtless thing to do. What if she had needed me? I left her alone in a big house. I said I was going to take care of her.

Phyllis took a sip of tea. "I think the proposal is amazing."

"How did the writing sound?" I asked, dying to be flattered.

"It was excellent," she said.

Of course, it wasn't excellent, but it was excellent that she said it was, and that bit of encouragement propelled me forward.

I had a book proposal—now what? The only person I remotely knew in publishing was the book editor I had met when I was fifteen years old and a patient in Payne Whitney, the woman I called Ellen the Editor. I met her my first night in the hospital where she was recovering from an alcohol binge. When the delirium tremens had passed, it turned out she was remarkably charming and fun to be with. Nearly ten years had passed since I had last seen her, yet when I called Random House, the publisher she worked for back then, sure enough, she was still there. I can't imagine what she thought when her secretary told her I was on the phone. She clearly wasn't happy to hear from me. She was tentative and evasive as I breathlessly rambled on about Marjoe and his forthcoming movie, and I begged her to let me drop my purple-prose proposal off at the front desk for her comments. She said no, they didn't accept manuscripts that way, it would not be read. But I pleaded with her, for old times' sake, two people who were once locked up in the loony bin together, just read it, only ten pages, not an official submission, please just tell me what you think, on and on until finally she said yes. I raced uptown to Random House and left a copy for her at the front desk.

Once Ellen the Editor was reading it, I decided I needed an agent to make a deal. But I didn't know an agent, so I called an acquaintance from NYU who was working as an assistant stage manager in a Broadway theater and asked him for the name of an agent. Since he was a theater person, he didn't know any book agents, but he did know of an agent named Shirley Bernstein who represented playwrights and lyricists, but not book writers. Still, perhaps her office could recommend somebody, she was very connected, she was the sister of composer Leonard Bernstein, and—

She was the sister of composer Leonard Bernstein.

Oh my God, Leonard Bernstein who my mother and I adored and who wrote the score to *West Side Story*. Shirley Bernstein *had* to be my agent. Whoever this woman represented, whether it was playwrights or lyricists or teddy bears, *she was Leonard Bernstein's sister.* I could hear myself saying, "Yes, my agent is the sister of Leonard Bernstein." I found her number in the phone book and called her office. I told her assistant, Patricia Fearl, that *Marjoe* was "under consideration" at Random House, and that I needed an agent to represent it. Patricia suggested I mail the proposal to the office, but I said I just happened to be nearby (well, I was home on West Eleventh Street), and could I drop it off in person? I think she took a liking to me and my naked ambition because she broke the rules and said yes. An hour later, freshly showered and dressed in a sport jacket and tie, full of charm and wild stories about Marjoe, the Miracle Child, I had talked my way past Patricia Fearl and I was sitting in Shirley Bernstein's office, the windows behind her overlooking Bergdorf Goodman's sunlit façade across the street on Fifth Avenue.

She was the most elegant Jewess I had ever met. I was dazzled by how regal she was, sitting catty-corner in her high-backed leather chair, a cashmere cardigan draped over her shoulders with only the top button buttoned, around her neck a single strand of pearls. She swiveled in her chair periodically to address her *éminence grise*, Doris Warner Vidor, the sexagenarian daughter of the movie mogul Harry Warner, and the widow of film director Charles Vidor. Doris was a fixture on the sofa, always impeccably dressed in a Chanel suit and clunky gold jewelry, either waiting to go to lunch with Shirley at La Côte Basque or just coming back from Grenouille, depending on when you caught them. When Shirley and Doris met Marjoe the following day at the office, he was at his most charming and high on the con. He was a smooth talker. The two ladies were so taken with him, he could have sold them a miracle handkerchief. Doris Vidor championed the idea of a book about Marjoe, as a latter-day Elmer Gantry. Shirley became inspired by the possibility of turning his life into a Broadway musical that her star client, Stephen Schwartz, would write. His new musical, *Godspell*, based on the parables of St. Matthew, was just about to open. So she agreed to try and sell my proposal to a publisher.

Only a week later Shirley Bernstein sold *Marjoe* to Frances Lindley, an esteemed editor at Harper & Row, who had edited Aleksandr I. Solzhenitsyn's *Gulag Archipelago*. Now she would edit *me*. We were paid $35,000 for the book, which I had to split with Marjoe. Since the publishers paid only half up front, my share on signing would be $7,875 after Shirley Bernstein's 10 percent commission, which I'm sure wouldn't even buy one strand of her pearls.

It was hard for me to believe. I woke up in the middle of the night bewildered. Was I having a dream? Did all this just happen to me? I was writing a book. I was writing a book. One day I was counterfeiting antiques at the auction gallery, the next day I had a book contract, money in my pocket, the redoubtable Frances Lindley was my editor, and I was writing a book.

Dr. Myers listened in amazement to the story of meeting Marjoe and getting the book contract. I could tell he was thrilled, despite his expertise at being a Sphinx. He was proud, too, deservedly. Getting a book contract for Marjoe was the accumulation of Wayne Myers's long-time insistence that nothing was impossible if I really wanted it, and that I could defy the odds.

When Howard Smith, the producer of the documentary, found out I was getting 50 percent of the book, he was furious that I'd insinuated myself into the project (and that he hadn't tied up the book rights himself). The next time he saw me, at a crowded party at Bromleyville, he shouted at me in front of all the guests that I was a "little hustler." He was wrong. I wasn't a hustler. I had seized an opportunity to move from being a survivor living on scraps, to having a place at the table. The proof of the pudding would be if it turned out I couldn't write a book. Then I'd be fired. Back to the auction gallery. But I wasn't going to get fired, because I was determined not to. I knew what I had to do. I had to learn to write. I quit the auction gallery again. I told them I was going to write a book. They placated me with a "Sure, sure," and Ziggy told me that my job would be waiting for me if I wanted it back.

What happened next was a testament to manic willpower. Without a plan, without a clue, I got on a plane and flew to California, where I conducted dozens of amateurish interviews with Marjoe's family and assorted people from his past. I did not know how to conduct an interview, or what I was really looking for. I was a twenty-four-year-old neophyte, in a rented car, tooling up the California coast for the first time, the radio on, Jackson Browne's "Doctor My Eyes" playing me through a very trippy journey. I smoked a lot of pot in cheap motel rooms before the interviews, and being stoned probably helped, because I taped long, rambling, curious conversations with my interviewees, which served me well in writing the manuscript.

I met Marjoe's mother in the lobby of the St. Francis Hotel and she was surprised by how young I was and the interview turned out to be more about me than her. On the way back east, I stopped in Texas and stayed overnight in the home of a Pentecostal evangelist introduced to me by Marjoe, who had no idea I was writing an exposé. I had never known people so relentlessly religious; in every other sentence there was a reference to Christ. When they quoted the Bible, I made believe I knew the passage. They were also openly anti-Semitic and I was petrified I was going to be discovered and they would do to me whatever it was they did to Jews. It was like being a secret agent.

When I got back with all the interview tapes, Phyllis's close friends, Evie and Dick Cohen, who lived on Park Avenue, gave us the keys to their weekend house in East Hampton and told me to get out of Dodge so I could concentrate on writing the book, instead of worrying about getting tickets to the next rock concert, or going to Max's. They thought that it might also be good for Phyllis to be out of the city, and that we could take walks together on the beach in the invigorating sea air, and at night sit peacefully by the fire. So early in the winter of 1972, I packed up my VW Bug and we drove out to East Hampton, where we holed up in a house in the Northwest Woods, while I wrote *Marjoe*.

As it turned out, there were no walks on the beach because the beach was freezing and nasty and Phyllis was frail. The winter days on the East End are not only brief, but they're colorless. A gray helmet hangs in the air like a bell jar, redeemed only by cold orange and icy pink sunsets that I could see through the naked lace of tree branches. The house we were given to stay in was modern and open, drafty not cozy, with knotty, raw wood walls and exposed rafters. The TV got only one station. We lit a fire and turned up the heat, but the damp was insidious. We touched each other a lot in the East Hampton house, a pat on the hand, an impromptu neck message, a hug, for reassurance, for affection, because we were scared. She was often distant, thinking things that she would not say out loud and that I had the good sense not to bring up. If I asked her, "Are you okay?" she would say to me, "Write the book."

In the mornings I went to the cozy East Hampton Library, and every day I chose a different biography, a person who would interest me. I would settle into one of the cozy nooks in a cul-de-sac with it. I didn't just read the biographies, I studied them. I took notes on the amount of dialogue, the order in which the story was told. I paid attention to how interviews were quoted to evolve the narrative. I even found out for certain whether the period at the end of a sentence belonged outside or inside the quotation marks. I read everything I could find about Pentecostals. I read Sinclair Lewis's *Elmer Gantry*. In the afternoons I wrote in longhand on yellow legal pads, sitting at the white pine dining room table, watching Phyllis doze on the sofa under a warm blanket. I wrote the book unafraid, with the confidence of a dreamer.

A month or more had passed when one night after dinner Phyllis became strangely lethargic. She was mumbling words like she was drunk and her eyes were drooping. I helped her into bed and asked repeatedly if she had taken her evening medication, but she was too loopy to remember. I dialed 911 and asked for an ambulance. In just a few minutes you could hear the siren, miles away out there in the still of winter, in the middle of the night.

The medics immediately gave her oxygen, and I explained she had Hodgkin's lymphoma and she was taking an assortment of medications, which I handed over to them. They were exotic cancer medications and none of the EMT guys knew what they did. One of them asked if she was my wife and I said no, she was my girlfriend, which was met with a confused frown. He asked to see her identification, so I went to her purse—Phyllis was very proprietary about her purse and I never looked in it—and I found her wallet and took out her ID. Before I handed it over to the medic, I looked at the date of birth and it didn't seem right. I did the math in my head. I was twenty-five and she was thirty-three, but the date on her ID would have meant she was thirty-eight, which couldn't be, because Phyllis was eight years older than me, not thirteen. I gave her identification to the medics as I did the math in my head again.

Phyllis's eyes fluttered and she tried to take off the oxygen mask but they wouldn't let her until she was alert, sitting up in bed. She insisted that she didn't need to go to Southampton Hospital. She had no idea what happened to her, but she was taking a lot of medication and she promised we would go back to the city in the morning to see her oncologist at Columbia Presbyterian. After a while the EMS packed up and left. I lay down next to Phyllis on the bed.

"I'm sorry I frightened you," she said, her eyes closed.

"I was scared," I admitted, and I held her hand until she fell to sleep.

I lay there thinking, eight years' age difference was okay, but thirteen years was . . . what? What difference did an extra five years make? It wasn't exactly like *Harold and Maude*, a most curious relationship between a nineteen- and eighty-year-old. What made me angrier? Was I more upset that Phyllis lied to me or that she was thirty-eight? God, she was *thirty-eight*. Wayne Myers was going to have a field day with this. Poor Phyllis. How could she live with that lie? How did she live with any of the crap in her life? Her life was so complicated and stressful and she was dealing with so many things, and on top of it she kept up a charade about her age?

In the morning she was slow and spacey, so we took our

time getting out of bed and I made her some tea and toast. We packed our stuff in slow motion and headed back to the city around noon. She stared out the window on the Long Island Expressway, past the exit where the lawnmower boy lived. We were listening to progressive rock on WNEW-FM when Rod Stewart's beautiful song "Maggie May" came on the radio. It was about an older woman who entraps a younger man, and it was at the top of the charts just then. I thought about nonchalantly trying to change the station, but that would have been too obvious, so I just let it play.

Oh no, she was crying.

"Please don't cry, Phyllis. There's no reason to cry."

"I'm crying because I lied to you," she sobbed, rummaging for a tissue in her pocketbook. "You saw my age last night on my ID. I didn't know how to tell you. It started when I fibbed about my age to Floyd, and by the time I got to know you, I didn't know how to correct it."

"I swear I don't care how old you are."

She cried some more.

"Please stop."

"I need to tell you about something else."

"Something more?"

"I had a nose job when I was seventeen."

A nose job.

"Now I'm really aghast!" I said. "I always thought your nose was too perfect. This is a terrible shock! You're a cupboard full of secrets!"

We began to laugh, from tension, and soon we dissolved into one of those hysterical out-of-control laughing fits that made me pull to the side of the road to compose myself. When we'd calmed down, we spent the rest of the ride in contemplative silence, and by the time we got to the city, she was wan and exhausted and I knew we had to head directly for the hospital. I drove her to Columbia Presbyterian's emergency facility, where she had been treated before. They said she had pneumonia and they admitted her. Late that afternoon her oncologist came by to say they had to first cure the pneumonia and get her strong again, before another round of chemotherapy. But he didn't seem very enthusiastic. I dozed in the chair next to her bed until a nurse woke me and said if I was going to spend the night, she would bring me a blanket, but I said no, I would leave. Phyllis was asleep but I whispered to her that I would be back in the morning and kissed her forehead.

It was cold outside but I was determined to walk home, even though it was five miles away and twenty degrees out. I started walking down Fifth Avenue and it struck me again for the millionth time that the city was beautiful at night and that I was in love with it, and happy to be a part of it, when the weight of what was happening fell on me. It was *horrible* to help somebody die. There was nothing noble about it. The truth was, I thought this thing with Floyd and Phyllis *was* a movie in the beginning. But in the script in my head the cancer never comes back, and I go off with Phyllis's blessing to be happily gay. She marries a handsome, rich Wall Street guy and moves to Rye, New York. But instead she was dying and I was a self-hating homosexual. Not the way I wanted the movie to end. Even if I wasn't up to this, I couldn't abandon her. I burst into tears on the street, my face all scrunched up, my nose running. People looked at me so I buried my head deeper in the collar of my ski parka and walked faster, and then faster, and soon I was trotting down the street, until I found an empty Yellow Cab and gave the driver the address not of the empty townhouse, but of Max's Kansas City.

A Visitation

That night there was an unusual viscosity to the smoky fog in the back room. The usual crew was there, whispering empty secrets about a hierarchy only they cared about, a set piece never ending. They made room for me at the round table, where I drank a few glasses of white wine. Somebody offered me a hit of coke off the knuckle of his forefinger. There was a young woman I knew from the music business, or maybe she was an artist, things were slippery that night, who sat next to me and asked if I had met Jon Wayne Lee, sitting across the table from us, smiling an empty smile. Jon was going to be Andy's new superstar, the woman said. He was from Texas via Boston, or so the story went, and somebody took him to New York and introduced him to Paul Morrissey at the Factory. They said he would replace Joe Dalesandro as Andy's Superstar, but nobody could ever replace Joe, the woman pledged, flicking her cigarette ash into a black plastic ash tray.

Jon Wayne Lee nodded at me knowingly from across the table. His teeth were so white, his smile was luminous. He was wearing a navy blue blazer with gold buttons, and he was handsome in a winsome, Protestant sort of way. He looked familiar. So familiar. When the woman sitting next to me stood up to go to the bathroom, he changed his seat and sat next to me.

"Do I know you?" I asked.

"Maybe," he said. He was such a good-looking man, but

there was something empty about him. He continued smiling at me, like he was radiating good vibes.

"Are you gay?" I asked him, searching his face.

"I'm not anything," he said.

"Do you mean you're asexual?"

"No," he said. "I'm very sexual."

"Why are you here at Max's tonight?"

"You asked for me," he said.

I laughed uncomfortably. "I didn't ask for you. I don't even know you."

"Don't you want me here? I can go."

"I don't want you to go," I said too quickly. "What do you want from me?"

"A cheeseburger."

I ordered him a cheeseburger. I ordered more wine.

"Do you always drink so much?" he asked.

"No. But you make me nervous. I feel that I know you from somewhere. How do I know you?"

He shrugged. My question was getting tedious. "I could be anybody and everybody," he said. When he was finished with his burger and got up to go to the bathroom, I could see that the back pocket of his midnight blue velvet pants was torn and I could see the skin of his right buttock.

I was drunk and high and we were in a taxi. The apartment smelled of Phyllis. There was a framed picture of us in the living room. Phyllis was hugging my chest and I was wearing forest green pants and a black turtle neck. "Who is this?" he asked.

"She lives here with me," I said.

"Do you love her?"

"I do."

"Are you going to cheat on her with me?"

"I am."

I led him down the narrow steps.

When I awoke, it was afternoon and he was gone. He left behind a note that said, "Take care of yourself because no one else will," along with a calling card that read, "Jon Wayne Lee." Later I asked about him at the Factory, but so many beauties passed through, they had no idea who he was. I asked about the woman he was with, from the music business, or maybe she was an artist, but no one knew who she was either.

Phyllis never returned to my apartment after that night. She was so ill that her family came up from Philadelphia to live with her, as she seesawed her way through several more recoveries and hospitalizations. When I asked one of her friends how Phyllis managed to deal with this and still be cheerful, she said, "Phyllis deals with this the way she deals with all bad things, like it's not really happening."

The last time I saw Phyllis was the following winter. She called to ask if we could meet for a cup of coffee. I told her that I'd meet her in front of the gym I belonged to on West 13th Street at 5 PM. Suddenly the gym and being in shape had become very important to me. Perhaps too important, but I had entered a new culture, and there were standards to be met.

It began to snow while I was in the gym, and when I went down to the lobby, the sidewalks were frosted white with a sugary topping. I stood just inside the big front window of the Health and Racquet Club watching the snow and waiting for Phyllis, but 5 PM came and went and she didn't show up. I began to feel guilty that I had asked her to meet me at the gym, instead of me just going to her apartment. What was I thinking? I started to imagine all sorts of terrible things, like her falling in the snow, so I went outside and paced anxiously on the street, until finally I saw her coming down the street, walking slowly, a stick figure in a black coat and hat, with a wool muffler around her neck.

I ran to her and wrapped my arms around her and kissed her. I kissed her forehead and her nose and her lips. I kissed her hat. Snow was sticking to her eyelashes. "Hi," she said, just like that first coquettish "Hi" at the Bleecker Street Cinema.

"Hi," I said back. She had a brave smile, but I could see she had lost a lot of ground. *I was thinking about what a friend had said and I was hoping it was a lie.* I stood there in the snow-hushed city, hugging, holding her to my chest, and when I looked up, the sky was dark and immense and scary, and I started praying.

She said she wasn't feeling up to having coffee, and she wanted to take a nap, so I walked her back to her apartment. We didn't say much on the way, we had said it all, I think, so we just held hands and looked in windows. When we got to her building, she said that she would speak to me in a few hours when she woke up, but she never called. As I walked home that night, the snow turned to rain.

A month later she sent me a note written with a purple pen in shaky handwriting, which sits before me now as I write this. It is entitled "MEMO," and it says, "Believing once you've ever loved someone, I believe I never said goodbye. I know it always embarrassed you when I told you that I love you, so I won't. Be happy. Phyllis."

This is what I learned from Phyllis. I discovered that I could love another person, and that I could love a woman, but not completely, and that I was driven by nature and design to love a man more. I learned I had to stop trying to love women and I had to stop trying to figure out why I couldn't, and I had to stop being ashamed of it. I found out that trying to love a woman would torment me because I would always have an eye out for the lawnmower boy. I learned that life was short and I had to get on with it, or I'd be left on the sidelines. I learned that my homosexuality was a complication, but not the engine of my life, and if I just let it be, I would be. And the last thing I learned from Phyllis would take a lifetime for me to know: She was the only person who would ever love me completely, even when she had everything at stake.

The Book *Marjoe*

The book *Marjoe* was workmanlike. The people at Harper & Row held their noses and published it in hardcover in 1972. Then a surprise. On March 27, 1973, the movie *Marjoe* won the Academy Award for Best Documentary of 1973, and Marjoe himself had fifteen minutes of fame. Even though the book had nothing to do with the movie, it got dragged along with the film's success. If my family and friends thought this was remarkable luck, no one was more stunned than me. Most important, I had published a book. I was in Payne Whitney when I was fifteen years old, and ten years later I had written and published a book. I slept with it under my pillow in my basement bedroom on Eleventh Street. I sometimes would wake in the middle of the night, filled with terror that I would come to no good, be nothing, nobody, and then I would reach under my pillow and touch my book and remember that I had written a book, no one could take that away from me. Even a hundred years from now, two hundred years from now, a dusty copy would be in the stacks of some library somewhere, a book with my name on it, and maybe someone will pick it up and read it and know that I was once alive.

PART TWO

Five Years Later

Gossip is mischievous, light and easy to raise,
but grievous to bear and hard to get rid of.
No gossip dies away entirely.
If many people voice it: It, too, is a kind of divinity.
—Hesiod, circa 700 BC

I would have missed my plane if I hadn't been awakened by
the rumbling of the furnace in the basement. It was an old
furnace, only six feet below my head, situated in the pit of a
coal boiler that was once used to heat the entire house. If the
furnace exploded, I'd be boiled like a bagel. I opened my eyes
slowly and peeked to the left, relieved to find that no one was
in bed with me. The night before, I had gone to Clive Davis's
Christmas party at Studio 54, and an evening at Studio usually ended with me under the influence of Rubell's Quaaludes
and free-drink tickets, then waking up the next morning with
God knows what in bed with me. Nobody even wants to have
breakfast the morning after a night at Studio 54. I was just a
teeny bit disappointed that I was alone. You never know, one
of those sleepy-eyed men of all shapes and sizes, colors, and
IQs, over the years, could have been a contender. But in the
morning light they all kept slip-slidin' away.

I could have happily snuggled under the down comforter

for another few hours but I had to catch the noon flight to Los Angeles. I forced myself out from under the comforter and walked naked and shivering up the creaky stairs to the kitchen, where I put water on to boil for instant coffee. There was no milk—the wheezing refrigerator, like a little white museum, was empty except for ketchup and mustard from Chinese takeout—so I gulped the coffee down black and lukewarm. At least it kicked my brain into gear. I came around under a hot shower. When I was shampooing my hair, I thought my scalp was bleeding, until I realized I was shampooing away flakes of red glitter, remnants of Studio 54 last night. I tried to remember who was there and what I did, but the glitter swirled down the drain like the contents of my mind.

Twenty minutes later, puffy eyed behind my aviator sunglasses, my perfect haircut still wet, I was dressed in a crisp white dress shirt, Levi 501s with the bottom button unbuttoned (a sign of eagerness in gay lore), cowboy boots from Frye, and a black velvet Yves Saint Laurent sport jacket gently worn at the elbows, so it wasn't too twee. I walked briskly down the front hall, dodging the white oak armoire as if it might reach out and grab me. The armoire had become a cornucopia of pain. Every morning a postman slid bills through a slot in the front door, and every afternoon I summarily deposited them in the overflowing armoire, until the urgency of having the phone disconnected, or my heating oil deliveries discontinued, forced me to take notice. I wasn't irresponsible, I just didn't have the money. My Gucci loafers had holes in the soles.

After *Marjoe*, I was offered a job editing a teenybopper rock and roll magazine called *Circus*. It was light on music and heavy on photos of rock stars with their shirts off. There were more nipples in *Circus* magazine than in any issue of *Penthouse*. *Circus*'s editorial was coordinated with advertising, which was coordinated with new album releases, so every cover was a positive feature about a group's new album, and every article had to start with the best anecdote about the new album, and end with the second-best anecdote. It was my own private hell.

I had been working for *Circus* only a few months when I heard that Lillian Roxon, who had published *The Rock Encyclopedia*, and wrote the *Top of the Pop* column for the New York *Sunday News*, died of an asthma-induced heart attack at a concert. Lillian Roxon was the godmother of all rock and roll journalists. Her *Top of the Pop* column was the most widely read rock column in the business. It was a powerful pulpit. The *Sunday News* then had a circulation of 1.8 million readers, and they were the only major newspaper in New York to have a regular rock and roll column.

I wondered, "Who's going to write her *Top of the Pop* column?" Somebody was going to do it. My grandfather told me that after World War II, housing was so scarce that people regularly read the obituaries to find apartments. Lillian Roxon was hardly in the morgue by the time I was in the *Daily News* building, the famous one with the huge globe in the lobby, where Superman worked, sitting across the desk from Lillian's editor, Shew Haggerty, pitching myself for the spot. I was soon handed an enormous amount of power in the burgeoning music industry, now a $2 billion segment of the entertainment business, grossing more than movies.

Regrettably, I didn't know what I was writing about. I didn't know if Gregg Allman played guitar or piano, or if it was Simon or Garfunkel who sang tenor. I had my own peculiar Bensonhurst taste in music. I was a sucker for schmaltz, violins, and introspective singer-songwriters who shared my dysthymia. I didn't listen to R&B; I don't think I understood it. In retrospect I was being racist. Then again, I never listened to greats like Lynyrd Skynyrd or Led Zeppelin either. To me, Neil Young was a divinity and Steely Dan the best music group in the world, ever. As for my writing skills, my columns read like high school book reviews. I was teaching myself how to write a newspaper column in public view. Perhaps my only achievement as a columnist was that I coined the phrase "Velvet Mafia," in reference to the Robert Stigwood Organization, a British record company and management group, and the term soon began to be widely used to describe the influential and nasty gay crowd who ran Hollywood and the fashion industry. Perhaps less to my credit, however enduring, was writing, "If white bread could sing it would sound like Olivia Newton John." I apologized to her later.

The problem with the *Top of the Pop* column was that it hardly paid any money. It wasn't even enough to live on paycheck-to-paycheck: $350 a month. Although I was flying back and forth between New York and Los Angeles like I was taking the subway, perks did not buy pizza or pay the electric bill. Still, I was in heaven; I would have done it for free. Anyhow, it was too late to do anything about the armoire that day. There were no armoires in Los Angeles.

There was a black limousine waiting for me in front of my house to take me to the airport. It was the same car and driver from two weeks before, although I couldn't remember what record company was paying for it. *The Nutcracker Suite* was playing quietly on the driver's radio. It was only six days until Christmas and the Nutcracker was haunting me like the clank of Marley's chains, but not as bad as "Little Drummer Boy," unless it was the David Bowie version. It was a lonely time of the year. The limo was passing a part of Queens that F. Scott Fitzgerald called "the valley of ashes." It was still ashen fifty years later, except instead of coal ash it was acres of gray fireproof warehouses and storage buildings, all the windows covered up, hiding whatever was in them. This was the curtain-raiser for visitors from around the world to a city in decline.

Living in New York in the seventies wasn't for the faint of heart. There was a whiff of something sinister in the air. The surfaces were hard, the streets were dirty, and a lot of gritty characters were about. Muggings were commonplace, cars were broken into so regularly that people put cardboard signs on their dashboards: "Radio Already Stolen." If you stopped at a traffic light, a drunken homeless man would appear from the dark and try to clean your windshield of the red lipstick kiss a tranny prostitute had left the block before. Everything was filthy. Payphones were breeding grounds for all sorts of plagues. I had to constantly wash my hands and clean my fingernails. There wasn't even a pooper scooper law until 1978.

As for it being the center of the arts, the longest-running film in Manhattan that year was *Deep Throat*. The Broadway Theater District was cheek by jowl with gay movie theaters and porn shops with jack-off booths. While audiences were watching a revival of *Hello, Dolly!* at the Lunt-Fontanne Theatre, across Eighth Avenue men were having gang-bangs in the orchestra of the Adonis Theatre. There were also, incidentally, a thousand different places for a gay man to get laid.

I never had any problems keeping my fingernails clean in Los Angeles. Whenever I boarded the plane at JFK, I told myself that if I kept my eyes closed during takeoff, a veil would fall behind me, obscuring the city along with the armoire, and the plane would pass through white cumulus clouds that filtered away the city's grime and abluted me of petty New York feuds and jealousies. At the LAX luggage claim, there was a man holding a handwritten sign that said "Gaines." I assumed he was the limousine driver, but instead of a limo, he led me to a short-term parking lot where there was an opal blue Mustang convertible with white seats waiting for me. The opalescent finish must have had twenty coats of paint; it looked like you could dip your hand into it. "It's a bit over the top," I observed.

"Not in Los Angeles she isn't," the man said, smiling.

"I don't even know who sent it," I said.

"I only drop them off, but you can call the rental company and ask."

I thought, perhaps it was better I didn't know. I tossed my bag in the back seat, put the top down, the radio on, and drove out of the airport onto the streets of Los Angeles, delirious with *dépaysement*. There was no reason to worry about what came next, or to fulfill my desperate need for approval. Everybody in Los Angeles was more desperate for approval than even me. Nobody seemed to work, and lunch was the most important part of the day. The songwriter and poet Elliott Murphy summed up his time in Los Angeles to me, "Swimming pools glisten while sunglasses listen to every word I say."

I drove high on palm trees and sunshine to the S&M, which is what Feiden called the Sunset Marquis Hotel. It was a trendy place, the Chelsea Hotel reimagined by Eve Babitz. The S&M had one-bedroom suites with kitchenettes, perfect for short-term residents, like young actors in Los Angeles shooting a pilot, or a writer fixing scripts, or the actor Van Heflin, whom I saw floating on a raft in the swimming pool. I stopped at the front desk to pick up my messages and a room key for 203, my favorite suite where Terry Southern holed up to write the movie *Candy*. (Everything has provenance in Los Angeles, every last barstool.) I changed into swim trunks and a tight T-shirt and went down to the pool, where I looked around for suntanned talent, hoping perhaps for a *cinq-à-sept* before dinner, but central casting was apparently closed. I dipped in the pool and swam a few laps before going upstairs to nap on the crisply pressed white sheets.

Two hours later I got up, showered again, dressed again, and the rest of the evening was a whirlwind of activity. I was picked up by Anni Ivil, the vice president of publicity for Atlantic Records. She had a Bardot pout and a Louise Brooks's haircut, except blond. She was petite but tough, a big spender. We were off to the Imperial Gardens on Sunset Boulevard. Just a month before, it was a tired Chinese restaurant, whose only distinction was that the space was once the Players Club, a movie star haunt in the 1950s that was owned by director Preston Sturges. For reasons no one could explain, except "That's Los Angeles," overnight it became the sushi/ chop suey joint *du jour* for the music business. As soon as we walked in the door, there was Ringo sitting at a table—not an animated character misplaced from *Yellow Submarine*. He kissed Anni on the cheek and shook my hand. I beamed.

I had just finished my Imperial Garden shrimp in lobster sauce and knocked back an Imperial Garden martini when Anni glanced at her small Tiffany watch and realized how late it was. We had to be at the late show at the Roxy, where a band called The Meatloaf was appearing, and Anni had promised his management that she would take me to see him. There was a flurry of activity as she called the waiter and paid the bill and we rushed out the door and jumped into her limo. When we got to the Roxy, it was high energy, lots of chummy press and music industry people glad-handing each other. When The Meatloaf took the stage, it turned out not to be *The* Meatloaf at all, but just Meat Loaf, a large man who was reminiscent of a meat loaf and who had a piercing voice and dramatic arrangements. He was so emotional and sweaty that his perspiration dripped on our stage-side table, and I had to put my cocktail napkin over my champagne glass. The show seemed to go on forever, although the audience loved him. The moment Meat Loaf finished his encore, Anni looked at her watch and like the White Rabbit, she said, "We're late! We've got to get to the studio!"

"The studio?" The studio. Of course. The whole reason for the trip to Los Angeles—the pearlized car, hotel suite, dinner complete with cameo by a Beatle—was because Anni Ivil had arranged for me to interview Peter Frampton and the Bee Gees at a night shoot of the *dreck* movie-to-be, *Sgt. Pepper's Lonely Hearts Club Band*. At that moment the Bee Gees had the number one hit song in the world, the goopy, middle-brow "How Deep Is Your Love?" Anni was besieged with interview requests, but she was giving the exclusive to me. Well, maybe not to me, but to the *Sunday News*.

"Of *course!*" I said, mustering enthusiasm. "*How Is Your Love?*"

"No," Anni said impatiently. "How *deep* is your love."

"Oh, *deep*," I corrected myself. In her limo, somewhere between the Roxy and the backlot of MGM Studios in Culver City, I began to fall apart in two time zones. It was hard to believe just that morning the rumbling furnace woke me. I admitted to Anni that I was fading fast and accepted an offer of a restorative. At the backlot we were greeted by the film's publicist and her assistant, chattering away as if perhaps they, too, had accepted a restorative. Anni and I were led on a tour of a cartoonish street of flats in Sgt. Pepper's Heartland. Most impressive, above us floated a giant hot air balloon with purple stripes and red hearts, lit by spotlights. I was escorted from trailer to trailer, where I pretended to interview Peter Frampton and two of the Bee Gees, who were all three tired and uninterested. Somebody should have offered *them* a restorative. No one seemed to notice that I didn't have a pen and paper and I wasn't writing anything down. Anni finally said we had to go, and she loaded me into the back of yet a different limo that took me to the S&M, where I wobbled through the lobby to my suite.

I let my clothes fall to the floor and climbed into bed, too stimulated to sleep, too drunk and stoned to stay awake. I exhorted Feiden's Haughty Dame Poof to come for me, but she was absent. I watched a light show play across the ceiling, reflected from the lights in the hotel's swimming pool. Somewhere, on another floor, a person was smoking a Gauloises cigarette on a terrace. It made me think of Floyd, how he always had a cigarette nearby during sex, and sometimes he took a long drag just before he came. The smoke thing was particularly odd because Floyd claimed his stepfather had molested him when he was young boy, and that the molestation only stopped when the man died of lung cancer. Now smoke was his fetish. I hadn't talked with Floyd in years. What would my life have been like if somehow I had managed to stick it out with Floyd? Not this? Not this life? Not this hotel suite? Would I have sacrificed my life for his? Followed him. How did his life turn out? The last I remembered, he had moved to San Francisco.

I would never actually call him, but I decided I would call information to see if his number was listed, just for the fun of it. I would never actually call him. Sure enough, there was a listing with his last name in a beach town called Pacifica, just south of San Francisco. It was a stupid thing to do, but I dialed the number, to see if his voice was on the answering machine. He picked up on the second ring, as if he was expecting a call at 2 AM.

"It's me, Glen," I said.

Confused pause.

"It's me, Steven."

"Wow. Hey, man, how have you been?"

I said that I was in Los Angeles, and I was thinking about him and the old days, and I thought I'd give him a ring.

"Those were *some* days," he said. I wasn't sure of what he was saying, good or bad? I could hear him striking a match and the sound of cigarette paper crackling as it burned. I could see his long fingers and bony knuckles holding his cigarette. I remembered the gentle pressure of his leg on mine in a dark movie theater. "The *miss*," he said. He still said that. It didn't mean he missed something; it meant good riddance, "The miss on that."

"There were *some* good times," I said, hoping he would agree. Some. Him striding down Eleventh Street, a dumb smile on his dumb pretty face, his Afghan dog hair flouncing with his stride.

"What do you do now?" he asked.

"I'm a *writer*," I said. "I was always a writer." I lied. Nobody is always a writer; they're always something else first so they can have something to write about. In my narcissism I expected he had followed my career.

"No fooling," he said, exhaling. "You *hated* writing."

Damn. The salient thing he remembered about me was that I suffered the chore of turning thoughts into words into sentences and paragraphs that would accrue to an article or column or book worthy of the reader's attention and a publisher to pay for it. It was daunting. "Well, I don't hate writing," I said. "It's hard, though."

"Yeah, I bet." He made a sound that was perhaps a commiserating chuckle.

"What are you doing now, Floyd? Are you still into photography?"

I hoped he would say he ran a photography supply store, and he was married and had two kids. "I sell used cars," he said.

I guessed that meant he was dealing drugs. I felt terrible for him; he had such a dead-end life. We wished each other good luck knowing we would never speak again and hung up.

Wouldn't you know, I felt that same yearning in my chest that I felt when he left the Greta Garbo Home six years before.

Comfortably Gay

There was one crazy moment when I was seeing three psychiatrists at the same time. I continued to see Wayne Myers on an irregular basis, and every other week I went to see a wonky psychiatrist who specialized in helping gay men be comfortable with themselves. He introduced patients to each other and gave cocktail parties and it turned out his practice was more of a hookup service for shy gay men. I also briefly saw another psychiatrist whose specialty was ridding gays of their "addiction." He recorded every session, but he was too cheap to supply the tape so you had to bring your own. You were supposed to listen to the tape at home, find the part you thought was most important, and then listen to that part every day until the next session. When he asked me to write the introduction to a book he was planning on how everything is an addiction, smoking, coffee, jogging, sex with other men, and I assumed, a psychiatrist who made you bring your own tapes, I quit seeing him. Finally I went to see the great homosexual witch hunter, Dr. Charles Socarides, the Dr. Mengele of the "homosexuality is a disease" contingent. He worked hard for a few weeks reinforcing the notion that I was sick before I quit seeing him, too.

In fact, I quit the whole cause. Curing homosexuality had become a moot point by 1973, when the American Psychiatric Association removed homosexuality from its official *Diagnostic and Statistical Manual of Mental Disorders*. The downside was that after a decade of analysis, I was filled with enough toxic self-hatred to kill ten men if I exhaled on them. The good news was that I was no longer sick or in need of a cure. Presto. According to the 1973 *DSM-II*, individuals comfortable with their homosexuality weren't mentally ill. Only those who were "in conflict" with their sexual orientation had a mental disorder. I was only sick if I was unhappy. But I *was* unhappy. I was bitter with my lot, misled by psychiatry about what was possible. *But you have to really want to change* was their hedge. Now I needed to find a way to be comfortably gay. Could I forgive myself for never having a flat stomach?

Thus I began an exponential shift into the life of an out gay man living in New York City, as I understood it, pretending to be happy, just like when I pretended to be straight. There I was on Greenwich Avenue, another face in the crowd. Another moustache. Another bomber jacket. Wandering the streets of the Village, rarely going above 14th Street. I saw the world through a prism with only one spectrum, gay, one goal, sex, stumbling through life as if in a sandstorm, too dense to see where I was going, too feckless to care.

Even on the hottest nights of the summer, I kept my window open instead of using the air conditioner so I could hear the city around me. I would wake up horny and sweaty. I would wiggle my nose like a predator who catches a scent of prey on the wind. It's just outside my townhouse door, down four steps, on the street. Unless you are of my kind, who would understand this? I slip into my jeans and T-shirt and slink out into the street. Gay Liberation's most immediate gift wasn't spousal health insurance; it was that gay men could enjoy massive doses of anonymous sex without reproach. There's something to be said for sheer sensation. If a huge amount of compulsive sexual experience was of any consolation, it was mine.

The most grievous casualty was love. Spoilsport Freud

questioned whether people could experience love and carnal desire at the same time. "Where they love, they have no desire. Where they desire, they cannot love," he wrote in "On the Universal Tendency to Debasement in the Sphere of Love." I had given up a great deal to be gay, but I didn't want to give up love. Prospectives passed through 146 West Eleventh Street like it was a stop on the IRT Seventh Avenue line. All sorts of people came to call. I loved the parade. It wasn't quite the Via Veneto, more like the Via Dolorosa. I was lucky I wasn't robbed or killed. There were plenty of unexpected moments like when I discovered a drug deal taking place in my living room, and one of the participants waved at me and said, "You only know me in my profession as a hairdresser." I didn't even know him as that. My friends couldn't believe the stories of the characters I met. Eventually a friend gave me a brass plaque to put on the front door that said, "The Greta Garbo Home for Wayward Boys and Girls." It was a lyric from an obscure song written by John Simon about a 1960s Haight-Ashbury hippie hotel in San Francisco, whose colorful residents included Jack, who lived in the back, of the "Greta Garbo Home for Wayward Boys and Girls." The plaque on my door was meant as a comment on all the lost beings who were in and out of my house. It wasn't a solicitation, but my next-door neighbor didn't understand it. He called me an "exhibitionist turkey" and stopped saying hello.

Topher

One night in early spring, when the city seemed to shrug off its pall, I was crossing Greenwich Avenue on my way to meet some friends for dinner when I ran into a neighbor, a painter, Stefan Cove, and he introduced me to his friend who had just moved to New York from Los Angeles, Topher Bloom. That wasn't his real name, but I promise you his real name was just as *trop mignon*. He was six years my junior, a Yale University dropout, chasing a romantic but uncertain career as a screenwriter in Hollywood. I'm a sapiosexual at heart; if you showed up on my doorstep with a degree from an Ivy institution, you could be 400 pounds and have polyps and I was yours. Of course, that was not the case with Topher Bloom. He had no polyps and he weighed 160. He had two personas. When he wore his oversized black frame eyeglasses, he had the open, wide-eyed appeal of a schoolboy at Eton, handsome but jejune. When he took off his glasses and wore a T-shirt and jeans, he morphed into one of those rugged guys you see on wilderness TV shows who can live in a tree. I studied every part of him, secretly, when he didn't know I was watching. I knew what each finger looked like, the shape of his earlobes, the tip of his nose. When he ran his fingers through his auburn-colored hair, it fell into the same perfect position. Occasionally a strand fell in his face, and he would flick it back into its place with a toss of his head. When we were alone and I had the chance, I kissed his hair, and it smelled like love and sex. See, they did exist on the same plane, on Topher's head. Just not in his heart.

How easy it would have been to spend my life with this charming man who'd gone to Yale, if only I was the man Topher was looking for. Alas, I wasn't tall enough or hairy enough, not Quentin Crisp's "great dark man" enough. I wasn't like the crazy marine in Topher's past, who had PTSD and riveted him to the mattress in animalistic fury. Perhaps my greatest failing in Topher's eyes was that I was smitten with him. When I looked at him, a halo of red hearts surrounded my head like a lovesick character in a cartoon. Topher found it quite annoying to be the object of my affection, yet he couldn't tear himself away. I worked on keeping him near. I plied him with everything I had. Kindness. Caring. Screenings. Backstage passes. Threesomes. Foursomes. ("Boys at play in the fields of the Lord," he whispered ecstatically during one of these adventure sessions.) When he mentioned in passing that he liked gray walls, I painted the bedroom gray for him. I introduced him to Andy Warhol, who photographed him nude. I even helped him get a book published. Topher had effortlessly written an outline for a trenchant novel about a young man and his two dogs, one who had cancer. I sent it to an editor I knew, and lo and behold, he bought it. It was only a $3,000 paperback deal, but now Topher was going to be a published author. "Everything happens around you, Gaines," he said, and I kissed his hair.

The one thing that was certain to happen around Topher was sex. Topher had frequent "adventures." He and I weren't officially a couple; we weren't officially anything except that we slept in the same bed. I once came home and there were bags of groceries spilled on the floor in the hallway that belonged to a man he had met in the pet food aisle at Gristedes. We didn't even have a dog. They were having an adventure in the living room. I was amused. Entertained. It was quirkily charming. Okay, maybe not amused or entertained, and not so quirky. I was confused about what I was supposed to feel, but I knew that if I tried to stifle him, I'd lose him. Later he sloughed off the incident with, "You should have joined us."

Was half a loaf better than none? Why couldn't I find a whole loaf? Was it because I was half a loaf myself? Or maybe I got it all wrong. Maybe sexual exclusivity wasn't the issue. Topher was exactly what I wanted; he was not a consolation prize. He was sexually impetuous, as he called it. I guess he had a lot more opportunities than most. Probably because of his hair.

Boschland

It was quite glamorous, in a *Day of the Locust* kind of way.
West 54th Street was a dumpy little cross-street in New
York's tenderloin district. Not much to see, a concrete municipal parking lot on one end, and a strip of down-market
Broadway stores covered in security gates on the other. In
the middle of the block there was a crowd of people spilling
onto the street from under the silver and black marquee. A
jumble of taxis and limousines, tooting their horns, blocked
54th Street all the way to 8th Avenue, and to intensify the
sense of urgency, a revolving emergency bubble on top of a
patrol car parked across the street splashed the crowd with red
light every few seconds. People were trying to get up to the
front, cawing like excited seagulls, "Steve!" "Steve!" "Steve!"
"Steve!" "Steve!" Some people jumped up and down to be
seen, or pumped their fists in the air, or waved wildly with
both hands like they were drowning. Every time the blacked-
out front doors opened, there was a blast of music and energy
from inside, stirring up the horde even more.

Hard to believe that a mob so passionate and eager could
be held back by a single red velvet rope. This now-famous
velvet rope was the demarcation between who was beautiful,
rich, famous, sexually desirable, and who was riffraff, trash,
unworthy of entry into a kind of paradise. The man who stood
behind the rope was an unlikely social arbiter. Steve Rubell,
twenty-eight, was a mouth-breather from Brooklyn, a short,
skinny man with thinning hair, and a big nose through which

he projected his voice over the din that surrounded him. When Rubell was stoned on Quaaludes, he sounded like a 78 record being played at 33⅓. The sweetest thing about him was his earnest enthusiasm for celebrities who came to the club. Every night he would recite the bold names in attendance with a sense of pride. He was a child with a toy. "You know who's here?" he would ask excitedly. "*Baryshnikov!*" The next most attractive thing about him was the plentiful supply of Quaaludes, the drug *du jour* that made you feel slippery and uninhibited. Rubell gave them away like Johnny Appleseed gave away seeds. Had it not been for a quirk of fate and luck, he would have been the manager of a steak house in Great Neck. (He had been.) Instead, he held one of the great powers known to man, the power of social validation. Or the power to humiliate. When you begged for admittance, Rubell held your ego in his hands. He blithely demoralized and easily embarrassed perhaps ten of thousands of people because they didn't meet his standard. He ruined the nights of people celebrating birthdays, anniversaries, a few Goodfellas, billionaire Arabs, and FBI agents. It's no joke to toy with someone's self-esteem. People hold those kinds of grudges for a long time.

Topher and I circled around the right side of the horde where there was a fire hose connection on the front of the building next door that I could step on so Rubell could see me over the crowd. I waved and he pointed me out to a security guard, who hauled Topher and me behind the ropes. Rubell grinned at Topher flirtatiously, which irritated me. "How you been?" he asked him, and I said, "I didn't know you knew each other." Rubell tried to diffuse any awkwardness by pressing a few free drink tickets into my hand plus four Quaaludes. The blacked-out front doors opened, and whoosh, music and lights and oceans of people swallowed me whole. I felt like I had just inhaled a popper and walked into a Bosch painting.

Studio 54, son of a bitch, was like mainlining endorphins. A former opera house stripped to its bones, it had a huge, gilded domed ceiling and a massive, crescent-shaped balcony that hung low over the orchestra. Everyone seemed ecstatic. People on the dance floor were flailing about in choreography from St. Vitus's Dance to Isadora Duncan. The music was too loud for anybody to talk normally and everywhere people were shouting in each other's ears. The bass pulsated through me, and I wondered if it could carbonate my blood and give me a stroke. The usual suspects, Liza and Halston were there, Elton John was on the dance floor, but he was just another face in the crowd, there were famous people everywhere. It was bedlam, this was the center of the universe, of somebody's universe anyway.

Nothing made me feel as good as holding hands with Topher, smiling in delight as I led him through the mass of people, holding tight so we wouldn't get separated, when suddenly, like a jump cut in a movie, Topher and I came face-to-face with Miracle Marvin Feld. I hated this guy. He was a married but closeted record company executive who I had written about in a *Sunday News* column. He had one of those terrible sloping nose jobs like the rich girls from Great Neck. I dubbed him "Miracle Marvin" in my column, a name I knew he hated. Miracle Marv had a gimmick, a knack of finding one-hit wonders from all over the world. He paid the acts a piddling amount, promising to manage them into a supergroup, then he made a fortune with their one hit and dumped the artists, who were never heard from again. There were lawsuits against him, a long list. But there was something else slimy about Miracle Marv, probably his $100 haircut and his big Columbia University class ring that he wore turned around so that it looked like a marriage band. When he saw Topher, his eyes lit up and he gave him a big disco hug with pats on the back.

What the fuck? "Good to see you," Marvin said to Topher, who looked trapped. "Let's get together!"

Before I could say, "How do you two know each other?" Topher took off into the crowd like a scared bunny. I would have set off after him, but Miracle Marvin grabbed me by the arm and pulled me close. He spoke right into my ear to be heard: "You should pick up your underwear on the floor next to your bed." It took me a second to process what he'd said, and when I fully understood, Miracle Marv smiled in satisfaction at the stricken look on my face. Marvin Feld had slept with Topher in my bed. Topher had sex with Marvin Feld in my bed. Miracle Marvin had seen how I lived, had seen my underwear on the floor, had probably looked in my medicine cabinet, had opened the night table drawer next to the bed that had lube and condoms and a cock ring in it. Had he looked in there? I would have looked if I were him. Had he taken a shower? I thought of the inside of my shower, the chipped porcelain, the used piece of soap on the ledge under the tiny window.

I will kill Topher. I will rip his head off.

Miracle Marvin turned his back and slipped through the crowd just like the slimy snake he was. My first instinct was to go after him and pummel him, but I was frozen in place, trying to compose myself. I thought, if we lived in Italy, I could shoot Miracle Marvin and get away with it. The Italians shoot their wives' lovers all the time. A crime of passion. I had to find Topher before I killed Miracle Marv. I fought my way through the crowd until I saw Topher standing near the dance floor, chatting with a man and woman I didn't recognize. "Follow me!" I ordered him. "Now! Immediately!"

He looked at me wide-eyed. He turned to the man and woman and said, "*Vous devez pardonner la grossièreté de mon ami.*"

He tried to introduce me, but I snapped, "I don't want to know these people." Mortified, the couple took a step back, excused themselves, and retreated to the dance floor, where they danced away from us.

"What the fuck is *wrong* with you?" Topher shouted. "Do you know who those people are you were so rude to?"

The crowd was making bird squawks to a song called, "Let's All Chant."

"You know what's wrong?" I shouted above the squawks. "You fucked Miracle Marvin Feld in my bed. *And he told me he saw my underwear on the floor!*"

Topher turned bright red, or maybe that was the disco lights. He rolled his eyes up to the heavens and blew out air with his lips fluttering like a squeezed balloon. "That guy is a *bastard*," Topher said. "A real creep."

"You're the bastard! In my own bed!"

"I'm sorry," Topher said. "You were in Los Angeles."

"Who cares where the fuck I was?" I shouted. "*You fucked somebody I knew through business, somebody I wrote about, in my bed!*" People around us could hear me. "Did he take a shower?" I demanded.

Topher looked at me incredulously. "I changed the sheets after, if it's of any compensation," he said.

"No compensation! No compensation!" I cried out. "Who else?" I restrained myself from taking him by the shoulders and shaking him. "Who else? Did you fuck Steve Rubell? Did you?" People were pushing past us and staring.

"I draw the line," Topher said to me, his spine stiffening. "If I chose to fuck Steve Rubell, it's none of your business, as long as it's not in your bed."

"My God, you slept with Steve Rubell!" I stopped restraining myself and grabbed Topher by the shoulders. "My God, you slept with Steve Rubell?" I shouted. It was a spectacle. Topher wrenched away and ran for the exit. By the time I caught up with him outside, he was already getting into a taxicab and I jumped in behind him. I cried loudly in the back seat, like a child, because this could never be undone. There goes the Topher dream. How could somebody I love disrespect me so much? My underwear would be a joke at a cocktail party. I was so upset in the taxi that Topher said to me, "Calm down, I'm afraid you're going to have a heart attack," but I continued to sob until I was hoarse. When we got home, I yelled and paced some more, and finally, exhausted by my own hysterics, I fell asleep at the dining room table with my head on a placemat. I was only vaguely aware that Topher packed and tiptoed out the door to make the first flight to Los Angeles.

The Count

That should have been the end of it, but every time I went to Los Angeles, Topher was there, somewhere. What were the chances I would run into him in Los Angeles? He probably lived in West Hollywood. Perhaps if I went to a popular West Hollywood restaurant? What would I do if I ran into him? Stop and greet him? "Oh, hello," cool but open-ended. Or would I walk by him like he wasn't there? That didn't make sense; I wanted to talk with him. Finally, I called his old landlord and tracked him down. (Okay, okay.) I said I was in town for the Bee Gees and asked him if he wanted to have lunch tomorrow on my last day in Los Angeles.

We met at the parking lot behind the Continental Hyatt House on Sunset Boulevard. Topher would park his ancient BMW in this unattended parking lot whenever he went off on an adventure in West Hollywood. He was wearing jeans and Top-Siders and a deep blue crew neck sweater over a white T-shirt, which showed around his neck like a clerical collar. He was tanned and his hair was a perfect mess. When he saw me drive up in the opal car, he smiled.

I don't know if I expected to shake hands or what, but I found us wrapped in each other's arms, rocking side to side a tiny bit, that kind of consoling hug people give to each other at funerals. He unexpectedly began to hug me even more tightly and nuzzled his chin into my neck and I nuzzled back. He felt so good, he smelled so good. "I'm sorry," he whispered.

"I did an awful thing. You didn't deserve that. You opened your home to me."

"I opened my heart to you, forget about the house." I gently pushed him away. I was surprised to see he had tears in his eyes. "It's all right," I said. I guess I was forgiving him.

Quickly distracted by the next shiny thing, he nodded toward the car. "What's this?" He was enthralled by the opal color. He walked all around it, caressing its lines and hollows. "Embarrassing, but perfection," was his verdict. He said he wanted to take a long drive, and he wanted to play with all the car's "features," he kept calling them, like the door speakers ("a very good feature") and the remote-controlled outside mirrors ("a luxury feature for comfort"), or bucket seats ("a feature to remind one how sporty the car is, despite being so middle-class").

Topher suggested we drive out to Point Dume to see the "Count of Turin." Topher had made the acquaintance of an elderly Italian gentleman who lived in a house on a bluff. He claimed to be the illegitimate son of the Count of Turin, who had died in 1946 without recognizing him. It was an improbable claim, but he told stories about his childhood in castles and palaces and poisonings in Capri. He told Topher that before World War II he grabbed all the family jewels, put them in a satchel, and stashed them in a Swiss bank, along with several million Swiss francs. After moving to the United States, he became head of the costume department at MGM. Now in his eighties, he was still, according to Topher, very handsome.

When we arrived at the house, he wasn't there, but Topher insisted we go inside and wait. It was a movie set. The walls were beachy white wood and every sliding glass door in the house was open; gauzy white drapes floated in the breeze. We wandered around the first floor looking at his things, framed photographs of him on an alpine ski slope, a note from a bridge tournament in Santa Barbara lauding his playing of the "fourth best lead." Also, a handsome curio cabinet, its regency style completely out of sync with the rest of the room. The cabinet shelves were filled with shiny bibelots and trinkets. There was a Bible with a pearl-studded cover, an eighteenth-century fireman's brass hat from Belgium, and a sterling silver set of an infant's comb, a brush, and a rattle. On the other side of the room there was an easel with a canvas on it, an unfinished painting of a palazzo paved in stones that looked like it had faded away, a dimming memory. There was a yellowed-with-age photograph of a beautiful boy from the 1930s, in a place that looked like Morocco. "I bet this was his lover," I said.

"I bet he had lots of lovers," Topher countered.

"I bet not. I think he's a long-term romantic kind of guy," I said. "Let's ask him when he gets here."

We found a white marble cigarette case on the coffee table with rolling papers and marijuana in it. "The count imbibes!" I said. Topher looked at me blankly. "It's a pun on a line from a movie, *The Big Lebowski*, you know, Jeff Bridges says, 'The Dude abides.'" I rolled a joint while Topher went behind the bar and fixed himself a gin and tonic, and me four fingers of vodka on the rocks. We sat on sling chairs on the deck just far enough apart so that if we extended our arms, our fingers could touch if we tried. We listened to the crashing of the waves. Soothing. We came from the ocean; it's mankind's first home. "The vast Pacific," I said. Topher didn't respond. "It's a line from a movie," I said. "Also Jeff Bridges. He says it in *Hearts of the West*, because he expects to be overwhelmed the first time he sees the Pacific, but he's not. He looks out over the ocean and solemnly says, 'The vast Pacific.'"

Topher smiled and nodded. Silence except for waves breaking.

I never want to forget this moment. I must remember this moment, on a chaise lounge next to Topher, close enough to touch fingertips, but we don't. I had a pang of nostalgia for the small things we'd shared, what seemed like inconsequential moments that turn out to be the richness of our relationship. We tried to change a tire on the side of the Montauk Highway but we couldn't figure out how to do it until eventually a Suffolk sheriff's vehicle stopped to help. One day Topher dashed off a painting on a canvas using stiff paint brushes that was so splendid we hung it in the hallway above the armoire. He bought a washing machine and paid to have it installed in the basement. ("It's the right of every American to have a washing machine," he told me.) I was proud to be with him, the way people looked at him as we walked down the street. I was proud of his Ivy League education, even though he never graduated. I'd never loved like that before. I must remember this moment, at the count's house on Point Dume, this metaphor of fingers nearly touching but not. "We write to taste life twice," Anaïs Nin wrote. "In the moment and in retrospection." The vast Pacific. Topher was wearing his Ray-Bans and the surf and beach were reflected in the lenses. The ocean glistened while sunglasses listened to every word I said.

"Topher, if you lose touch with me, will you remember that I said writing is hard?"

"What is the matter with you?" Topher asked softly.

"I'm having a bad nostalgia trip."

"Jesus. You know what they say—you can look back, but you can't stare."

"That's AA," I told him.

"AA took all the good sayings," he grumped. "Just relax and enjoy the vast Pacific."

I watched a jogger down below running on the beach with zinc oxide on his nose. He was shirtless and yet it was the end of December. Fucking endless summer. "How can this be Christmas?" I demanded. "Los Angeles is the antichrist of Christmas—warm weather, blue Christmas trees on Wilshire Boulevard, fireplaces with gas flames. Santa would never, ever come here."

Topher nodded his head slowly, like he was digesting one of the most important things he'd ever heard. Either that or he was a thousand miles away. I'd guess a thousand. We were silent for a time. I looked at my hands, my clean fingernails. I had a desire to lean over and kiss Topher's hair. "Do you think we choose who we love?" I asked. "Or is it just pheromones?"

"Fix yourself another drink," he said. "It's an open bar."

"What are you planning to do for Christmas?" I asked. "Do you even have a Christmas tree?"

"No," he said, looking at the runner on the beach, who had suddenly caught his attention.

"Of course you don't. *I* have a tree," I lied. "It's out on the back deck of the townhouse. Ten feet tall."

"You do not," he said.

"And I'm going to see the Rockettes," I lied again. "I have tenth row tickets. I know you love the Rockettes in case you want to come."

"I do not love the Rockettes," he said. There was contemplative quiet. "Are you inviting me to New York for Christmas?"

"I could be. If you come with me to the Rockettes and don't fuck anybody in the cast."

He was quiet again. I was afraid I had crossed a line, but instead he grunted, "No promises."

"Did you kiss Miracle Marv like you kissed me?" I asked.

"Oh my God! Not this again. Is this why you wanted to see me today?" He cleaned the lenses of his sunglasses with his shirt. "I don't remember kissing *anybody*."

"Not even me? You must remember kissing me, every part of me."

"Do you know what your problem is? You're so fucking *intense*. Do you even *realize* how intense you are? Let go of shit." He drank down the last of his gin and tonic, spit an ice cube into the glass, and got up to get himself a refill.

"Why do you have a hard-on?" I asked him. I could see it through his jeans.

"See! You *are* so intense."

I got out of my chair and tackled him, wrestling him to the floor. After, Topher suggested we go upstairs to see if perhaps the count had had a heart attack and was lying dead in his bedroom. He wandered through the house calling, "Vittorio? Vittorio?" and I followed him, calling, "Count of Turin, where are you?"

Topher went to a room at the end of the hall and stood in the doorway. "Hey, come here and see this."

It was a big room, half the size of the whole first floor beneath it, with six tall windows facing the ocean. There were mannequins everywhere, dozens of them, in different poses, some stiff, some caught in mid-action, each with impeccable makeup and individual hairstyles. They were dressed in evening gowns and they all had small tags affixed. One said "Greta." One said "Rita." One "Lucy." Another "Veronica."

"These are real," Topher whispered, as if the mannequins could hear. "These are real movie star dresses. This whole room of gowns must be worth a fortune."

I wandered among the models and read the labels out loud. "Lana. Hedy. Grace."

There was a framed photograph on the wall of a man with a goatee and two stripes of gray in his hair, dramatically swept back from his temples. He could have been a Munster, except he was dressed in the cream-colored "Lana" gown. He was slim and I thought it fit him rather well. There was another photo of the same man in the gown marked "Gloria." In this photo he was in full makeup, wig, and jewelry.

"The count, I presume?" I asked Topher.

"Well, I'll be . . ." he murmured, studying the photos. "Good for him."

"It's remarkable how much the count can look like Gloria Swanson, even with a goatee." I peered at Topher. "Did you sleep with the count?"

He shook his head, not to mean "no," but in wonder. "You never change."

"No, *you* never change."

I thought I heard a car door slam. "We must go downstairs," Topher said. "If that's him, I don't want him to find us up here."

We tiptoed out of the room and hurried down the steps. The car door slamming we heard was in the driveway of the house next door, but we decided to leave anyway before the count came home. Topher found a yellow legal pad on the kitchen table, and we left a note, saying we were sorry we had missed him and that we'd be in touch. We were pretty much silent on the drive back to town. Neither of us reached to turn on the radio, although Topher did approve of the AM-FM stereo sound system as a "winning accoutrement." It was dusk by the time I dropped him off in the lot behind the Hyatt House. I got out and hugged him.

"Merry Christmas and Happy Chanukah," he said. We hugged again, tightly this time, and I took a deep breath of him.

I watched as he drove away until his car got lost in the traffic on Sunset Boulevard. I thought I had put a period on the end of that sentence, but when I got back to the S&M, Topher called. "What time is your plane tomorrow?" he asked. I told him American Airlines at noon. "I'm going to book a seat and spend Christmas with you," he said.

I got a little choked up, which I knew he would hate, so I pretended I was coughing, but I couldn't hide that I was happy to be spending Christmas in New York with Topher. I offered to pick him up in the opal mustang and he could drive it to the airport, but he said no, he was going to dig out his ski parka for winter in Manhattan, and that he would meet me at the gate at LAX.

But he never showed up at the gate. I searched the terminal, hoping to see him emerging from the crowd of Christmas travelers, hoping that we'd embrace and the camera would spin around us like the end of the Claude Lelouch's movie *Un Homme et une Femme*. I was humming the theme music when they announced the final call to board the plane. I went inside and a few stragglers showed up, but it wasn't until the plane door closed with a thud and a hiss that I gave up hope. I sort of expected it. I wasn't wildly upset. Okay, maybe. When I got back to New York, there was a message from Topher on my answering machine. He said he was sorry, but he had a late night, an unexpected adventure, and he wound up in the Valley and overslept. He couldn't help himself. The miss on him.

Like An Eagle

Jacques Morali, the inventor of the Village People, was a goosy, Moroccan-born Jew, shaped like a pear, with a pouty mouth and a flaccid lower lip that threatened he might drool. He was hopeless with the English language, which he tried to speak by pronouncing words syllable by syllable, contorting his mouth into unusual shapes while trying to finish a sentence. Morali became of interest to *New York* magazine because he was thinking about selling the Village People to a large entertainment entity, like you would sell a sports team. Morali had invented the characters in the Village People from a cocktail of gay stereotypes that comprised his sidewalk fantasies. He also invented The Ritchie Family—who weren't sisters or named Ritchie—with a hit disco update of the 1939 song "Brazil." He planned to create a cottage industry of composing and producing hit records with fabricated groups.

When *New York* magazine published the article I wrote about him, extolling his composing and producing abilities, Morali was thrilled. He called to thank me, saying, "I'm going to make you reeeech."

"What?" I asked.

"Reeeeech. *Mun-ee. Reech.*"

"Oh, *rich! Money!* How?"

"You are going to write the lyrics for my next album."

"Wow!" I exhaled a blast of pot smoke. A hit disco album *could* make me reech. "What is your next album?" I asked.

"*C'est le début de mon amour*, Dennis Parker."

Oh no. Morali met Dennis Parker through a sex ad in the *Village Voice* (no Internet back then). Parker's real name was Wade Nichols (perhaps). He made straight and gay porn films, including *Bang Bang You Got It* and *Boy Napped*. He was slickly attractive, with a ski-jump nose job, strong chin with a cleft, and a big brush of a moustache covering his upper lip. Morali *loved* moustaches. "*Moo-stashes*," he called them. He told me many times that Parker was the best sex he ever had, and curiously enough a year or so later, a Studio 54 bartender, Robert Jon Cohen, told me the same thing. "I don't know what he did to me," Cohen said, rolling his eyes. "But he was the best sex I ever had."

What he did to Morali was fist-fuck him. I know this unfortunate detail because when I went to interview Morali for *New York* magazine, he proudly showed me around the apartment he rented in a new condo tower within arm's reach of the Queensboro Bridge. When he brought me into his plush, over-decorated bedroom, he said proudly, "This is the bed where my boyfriend fist-fucks me."

"How nice," I commented, not sure of an appropriate response. The bed had a beautiful suede headboard. "How do you manage not to stain the headboard?" I asked.

Morali glared at me indignantly. "What do you think we are, *pigs*?"

Morali had already picked out the title of the song for which I was writing the lyrics, "Like An Eagle." I asked him what was he trying to evoke with the music, and what did the song mean to him?

Morali's voice broke when he reminisced about the first time he was on his knees in front of Dennis Parker. Dennis had an eagle on his belt buckle.

I was writing a song inspired by a blow job.

Morali gave me a tape with him singing sounds instead

of lyrics, like he was being examined by a doctor. To give him credit, aside from his la-la-las, he had written a beautiful, haunting melody. I was inspired. I thought I was going to be a disco Stephen Sondheim. To show off, I wrote the lyrics with inner rhymes and repeating imagery. Frankly, they were cheesy, but so was disco music. A week later I met with Morali in the recording studio, along with Dennis Parker and some of the Village People, who were hanging around in the control booth. I sat on a tall stool in front of a microphone and put on headphones. I was terrified.

The music began to play and in a shaky voice I sang the heartfelt lyrics to my masterpiece. I remember only fragments of the lyrics now, and that I got stuck on the word "insatiable." There are very few words that rhyme with "insatiable" appropriate for a disco song about an eagle. ("Fungible" is one.) I wanted to write a song about the search to sate a desire that was insatiable. I wrote about a man whose life was overshadowed by this need. I was only halfway through the first stanza when Morali had a tantrum. Considering I had sung only twelve words, and not run over his dog, I thought his explosion was a little big. I didn't know if he was putting on a show for everybody or if he really *hated* the lyrics that much. "*Tooo compliqué!*" he shouted. He tried to say the lyrics aloud in his thick French accent but only ended up spitting all over the room. Morali said that I was an amateur and the words were impossible to sing, and that people who were high on a dance floor didn't want to listen to all those words, they needed to hear a simple phrase *répété*. The Village People were snickering in the control booth.

Morali said he would cut down my lyrics himself, and that I should come back the following week to hear the finished song. I sat in the control room and listened to the new improved lyrics: "*Like an eagle, like an eagle, like an eagle, like an eagle, like an eagle,*" about three dozen times, with a few cloying "searching" or "wanting" words thrown in, and a high pitched "*I fly,*" which also could have been "I cry." I could tell it was Morali, not Dennis Parker, singing. Morali added soaring computer-generated violin lifts, "popper breaks" as they were known in the trade when the dancers would take a snort of butyl nitrite and soar along with the synthesized violins. Even with the dumb lyrics and overly dramatic production, the finished song had a haunted quality that captured the longing and eternal hunt for prey. With all the layered tracks and synthesized instruments, Dennis Parker's voice was barely audible, but he wasn't there for his singing. There was a photo of his eagle belt buckle on the back of the album cover.

Morali and Casablanca Records "debuted" the song at Flamingo, Manhattan's membership gay dance club. It was hard-core, open only Saturday nights in the winter when Fire Island was deserted. To get a membership at Flamingo, you had to audition by going to the office at an inconvenient time in the afternoon, wait in a long line, lift your shirt for the guy behind the desk, and tell him what sign you were. There was no alcohol at Flamingo, everybody was on drugs, and they served only juices and water to keep the dancers hydrated. By daybreak on a cold and dreary winter's Sunday morning, the windowless Flamingo was packed with 500 sweaty men stoned on various chemicals, eyes half closed, bobbing and writhing, their T-shirts tucked into the back pockets of their jeans, right pocket for bottoms, left pocket for tops, tucked in the middle if you didn't care. The dancing was frenzied, no pretensions to form, like at Studio 54, these guys were looking to dance themselves into a hypoxemic heap. It wasn't my cup of tea, but I wanted to be part of whatever it was that I was supposed to be part of, so I went, especially to hear "Like An Eagle" played in a disco for the first time.

I recognized the song's opening whooshing sounds of wind and synthesized strings and immediately the crowd was whooping and waving their fists in the air in approval. I wanted to enjoy that moment. Okay, I wasn't Stephen Sondheim, and Morali wasn't Leonard Bernstein, but still, I tried to be as present as one can be on the drug *du jour*, but my thoughts went awry and I thought about the armoire, and when all the men raised their arms up in the air, so everyone could see their biceps, I did too, and I tried to savor the moment, to be in the moment, but I wasn't comfortably gay, and just then somebody held a bottle of butyl nitrite called Rush under my nose, and when I pulled away not to smell it, he accidentally spilled some on my moustache. Then I couldn't stop breathing it. I should have bolted for the bathroom and tried to wash the chemicals out of my moustache, but I was already spinning like a gyroscope, and there was a chorus of ethereal voices commiserating with me, *gonna getcha, gonna getcha*, and the dancers seemed to enjoy it. So instead of washing the chemicals out of my moustache, I danced on. My blood vessels dilated, my blood pressure dropped, my muscles turned gummy. I danced on. I wanly waved my hand in the air and tried to hear the lyrics but there was a delay between me and the music, and I imagined I was looking down at the writhing pit from far above and trying to find me among the dancers. But I was indiscernible from all the other men. I was comfortably numb.

When the song was over, I went to the bathroom and washed my moustache as I could, and left Flamingo. I walked home half-high on butyl nitrite, killing millions of brain cells. I shaved off my moustache for the first time in ten years to get the stink of the whole experience off me. I heard "Like An Eagle" a dozen times after that, in dance clubs and gay bars and radio stations. Any time I hear it, a big gray hand comes down from the sky and pulls me back to the end of the seventies.

The only pleasure the song ever gave me was that I have this story to tell.

It turned out Jacques Morali didn't make me reech. I was paid only a pittance for "translation rights," supposedly because I translated his lyrics from French. In any event, Morali quickly bored of me, which was fine because he was quite tedious. He moved on to the next *moos-stache*. As our friendship drifted, he turned inexplicably mean. When I ran into him one night at Studio 54 and told him that I had a cold, he said, "I'm too important to be sick." Unfortunately, that was not true. There was no HIV test at the time, so it was a crapshoot if you were infected. Morali was already morbidly hypochondriacal. It destroyed Morali when Dennis Parker was diagnosed with Kaposi sarcoma and shot himself in the head in 1985 at age thirty-eight. With Dennis gone, Morali spent the last six years of his life in misery. Every sniffle, every pimple on his face, sent him screaming off to the doctor's office. Even disco deserted him, a craze that died with its dancers. Morali passed away of AIDS in a Paris hospital on November 15, 1991.

Disco Sally

When I got sacked from my column at the *Sunday News*, the editor of the entertainment section tried to console me, saying that having a column for almost four years was "a very good run." Not so. People write columns for many years and make fame and fortune from it. Truth was, I was bored of deadlines, bored of rock and roll, and my columns had degraded in quality, having not started from a very high standard to begin with. The afternoon I got fired, I went to a screening of a new movie called *Saturday Night Fever*. I was in the elevator going up to the screening room in the Gulf & Western Building along with a music business publicist and a young rock writer named Cameron Crowe. He was smart and talented, a pimply sixteen-year-old kid from California who had been making a name for himself writing major pieces for *Rolling Stone*. I told him that I had been fired from the *Sunday News*. "Well, did you think you were going to be a rock critic for the rest of your life?" he asked.

I never expected to be a columnist to begin with. But now that I'd lost it, I felt powerless. "Aren't *you* going to be a rock critic for the rest of your life?" I asked Crowe.

"No, I want to direct movies," he said.

Fat chance, I thought.

Was I naive to be surprised that after I was fired, I was removed from screening lists, backstage passes, and soon the restaurant maître d's and club doormen no longer recognized me? I had convinced myself that, aside from my column, they really liked *me*, not just my byline. They didn't. The wellspring of perks turned to a dribble. Of everything, my greatest fear was that I would lose my ultimate privilege, free and unfettered access to Studio 54. When I arrived at the red velvet ropes the night I was fired, Rubell seemed excited to see me. "*You got fired!*" he cried out, trying to look as sad and sympathetic as possible, what with all the muscles in his face slack from Quaaludes. "What are you going to do now?" he asked me gravely.

"Did you think I was going to be the *Top of the Pop* columnist for the rest of my life?" I asked him. (Thank you, Cameron Crowe.) While Rubell was trying to process this, I cut to the chase. "You're still going to let me in here, aren't you?"

I could almost see the drug-wasted synapses in Rubell's brain try to fire up behind his eyes. What he wanted to say was, "No, I don't want to let you into Studio 54 for free and fill your pocket with drink tickets and Quaaludes anymore, because not only did I fuck your boyfriend, but yesterday you had a bully pulpit with nearly two million readers and today you have a readership of zero."

Instead, he said, "Yes, of course I will let you in." I was touched, considering he had cuckolded me. I hugged him, because entry to Studio 54 was more important to me than my dignity. Rubell kept his promise and continued to welcome me with hospitality and warmth. I did not repay him in kind.

With about $50 in the bank and a chip on my shoulder, on October 25, 1978, I pulled myself together at Eleven PM and went to Disco Sally's 78th birthday party at Studio 54. Sally was a crepe-papery septuagenarian who wore sunglasses and skimpy outfits. She was a widow and former attorney who danced with shirtless young boys like she was a cheerleader, throwing her legs up in the air. People loved it. "Isn't it wonderful that at any age you can defy expectations and have fun, like Disco Sally?" they asked. No. I thought she was being exploited. I felt bad for her, although she was probably a lot happier in her life than I was in mine. Her birthday was obviously a big deal because the place was a madhouse. All the night crawlers were there, basking in their own limelight, ecstatic to be part of a party for Sally.

I cashed in my last free drink ticket for another vodka and slapped a $5 tip on the bar for a shirtless bartender who danced in a circle while he poured my drink. I headed up a carpeted flight of steps to the mezzanine lounge, where the lizards were smoking cigarettes and chittering away. On either side of the mezzanine were two large polysexual bathrooms, busy as beehives with people going in and out of the stalls doing restoratives, and possibly each other. Few people used the stalls for their intended use. While I was using the urinal, I saw in the mirror that my friend Tinkerbell was reattaching a false eyelash at the sink. She was a knockout, a blond sylph dressed in a slinky sequined dress. We were good friends, on and off, but she was unpredictable. She projected a very fragile affect when she wanted to, but in the same little girl voice she also packed a razor-sharp wit and a vocabulary like a truck driver, so the banter could turn rough. Mostly she was funny. I remember her asking Peter Allen, "So who is the one man in your one-man show?" Her real name was Veronica Visser from Scarsdale, long forgotten by those who knew her because people were much more entertained by the witty Tinkerbell persona. She wrote for Andy Warhol's *Interview* magazine, had a brief stint as the film critic for WNEW-TV, and she was writing a long-awaited memoir, *Sometimes a Somebody*, which, like Penelope's weaving, never got done. I read the first page once. It opened with a cab driver asking her where she was going, and Tinkerbell answered, "Crazy, and step on it."

"Are you holding?" Tinkerbell asked me.

"I'm never holding," I said.

"You're in luck," Tink said. "Follow me."

I shouldn't have been surprised to discover that the stall she led me to was being guarded by her beautiful brunette apartment mate, Jayne Fredricks. The three of us crowded inside the stall and locked the door. Jayne threw her arms around me and kissed me hello. She was high. "What are you going to do now that you got fired from the *News*?" she asked.

"Will we find you selling pencils on the corner?" Tink asked.

"Maybe you'll see me behind the counter at Bloomingdale's tie department."

"The first floor, it's a good location," Tink said. "You'll get to see plenty of old friends go by."

"Can I ask you a personal question?" Jayne said, putting her hand on my arm and squeezing. "Do you kiss somebody before you fuck them in the butt?"

Oh. "Do *you* kiss them before they fuck *you* in the butt?" I asked.

"During," she said, unruffled. I believed her. She produced a screw top bottle with a spoon attached to the cap. It was brimming with cocaine.

"Where did you get all this?" I asked.

"She let a man eat her pussy and he gave it to her," Tink said. "It's like Jayne is a Bond girl—Goldpussy." She passed around the restorative and Tinkerbell said she was worried that she was really losing her mind, no joke. She said the devil had come into her bedroom last night. "He didn't even knock," she said. She blinked her big blue eyes at me. "I said to him, 'You call that an outfit?'"

"Wow, you questioned the devil's fashion sense? What did the devil say?"

"He said, 'It's been a tough year for devils.'"

Only Tinkerbell had hallucinations with punch lines. I said maybe Tinkerbell would stop feeling crazy if she laid off the coke, and she told me maybe I would feel less crazy if I laid off the cock. I said I enjoyed joining them in the Studio 54 holy ritual of cocaine in the bathroom, but I really had to be on my way. I left them in the stall with that huge bottle of "the only thing that matters." They should just rent out one of those stalls and live there.

I walked through the lounge and up another flight of stairs to the balcony. Most people went up there to have sex, which was why they covered the floors in rubber tiles, so they could wash them down more easily in the morning. I went up there to be alone, to be separated from the scene below. Just watching was meditative. It was an imposing sight from up there, people writhing on the dance floor, a big amoeba of people bobbing up and down, thinking they were having the best time at the best place on earth to be at 1 AM on a Thursday night. Don't these people have jobs? Why did I resent their pleasure? Was I jealous of Disco Sally? Perhaps I just stayed too long at the fair, too much of a good thing, although Studio 54 wasn't exactly a good thing. It wasn't that my nose was pressed up against the window of a bakery; I had been allowed inside, I just couldn't eat. I couldn't compete in fame or fortune to participate fully. Studio 54 was a high school cafeteria. Maybe everything in life was a high school cafeteria.

When I left Studio 54 that night, the relative quiet of West 54th Street was a relief. The crowd had dissipated, the velvet rope had been rolled up, and there were only a couple of rejects milling about along with a few cops and trannies. I recognized one of the bartenders, dressed in a black undershirt, leather jacket, and jeans, sitting on a motorcycle at the curb like some bad gay porn setup. He revved his engine at me. "You're the rock and roll writer, right?" he asked.

"I *was* the rock and roll writer," I said.

"You sound drunk. Are you drunk?"

"A little."

"I know how to sober you up," he said.

"What's that?"

"A ride home on a motorcycle."

"I think I'd fall off the back."

"No, you won't. You'll be holding on to me. Where do you live?"

"I live on Eleventh Street. Hey, how old are you?"

"I'm twenty-one. How old are you?"

"I'm thirty-one."

"You're old enough to be my father," he said. "Come on, hop on the back and I'll take you home."

I climbed clumsily onto the seat behind him. When he told me to wrap my arms around his chest and hold tight, I hadn't realized that I would be pressed up against him like that. I closed my eyes and melted into him like Silly Putty. There was no helmet law then, and the speed and danger were frightening, the ground falling away beneath us as we sped down the empty streets at three in the morning, so fast that the traffic lights smeared as we went by. I'm not sure what happened in bed with Robert that night, but I never quite recovered. It was like crack or meth—once you try it, it sets a standard for a new high. In a world where he might otherwise be one of the crowd, he had a gift. He was very good sex. Or maybe all twenty-one-year-olds are very good sex. (As it would turn out, he was really twenty years old, but he also lied to Steve Rubell to get the job bartending.) Robert loved to be adored and he was indeed adorable. At dawn we sat on the bed naked, smoking joints. His hair was jet-black and curly, and he had long eyelashes, like an ostrich. There was one part of him that I found the most thrilling, a triangular patch of dark hair between his pectoral muscles. I kept being drawn to it while he lazily told me how he moved to New York, a skinny kid with bad skin from Miami Beach. When he first got to New York, he tried to get a job in the fashion industry as a belt designer. He was the only person I ever met who aspired to design belts. He also started to lift free weights at the Sheridan Square Gym, an old-fashioned place that catered mostly to straight, hard-core bodybuilders. The regulars were all helpful to the skinny kid from Miami who worked out so hard. I don't know if it was perseverance or DNA, but he filled out in a very appealing way, not like another gym musclehead.

Robert told me that the first night he went to Studio 54, he waited in the crowd out front, feeling insignificant, worried about his acne, when Rubell spotted him and beckoned him in. He was gay catnip. Whatever bar Robert was behind that night, he earned the highest grosses, and he got the most tips of any bartender. People just liked to look at him. He was sweet and warm, but indiscreet, full of stories about Studio 54—the money hidden in the ceiling of the basement; the cash register tapes changed in the middle of the evening to help cook the books; Steve Rubell masturbating over piles of cash he brought home to his apartment in a shopping bag; the ejaculation-distance contests in the basement, the most distant shot winning an invitation to St. Barths for a weekend. He also told me one by one the fetishes and peccadilloes of every prominent person he had slept with. Robert said the first night he met Halston, the designer came up to his bar, ordered a drink, and then ordered Robert. Much, much later that night, after a few grams of coke and a bottle of iced Stolichnaya at Halston's townhouse at 101 East 63rd Street, Robert was hired as Halston's personal assistant so he could learn the ropes of the fashion business. Unfortunately, Robert's naïf charms and bedroom savvy didn't translate to the showroom, and he soon lost his appeal with Halston, who passed Robert down through the ranks of the Velvet Mafia. "That gay crowd thinks they pass the bartenders around," Robert told me. "But the truth is, we pass *them* around." If I was being passed around, so be it. That night I cheerfully took my place in Robert's food chain. He slept in my arms, waking me for sex every three hours like a baby who wanted to be fed.

While he was asleep, I went to my office and sat in front of the same Smith Corona Coronet portable electric typewriter on which I had written the *Marjoe* proposal, and wrote the same words: "There are hundreds of them out there every night . . ." Only in this version when the crowds came "from the flat plains of the Midwest," they didn't come to see the "Miracle Child," they came to be part of the most famous nightclub of all time, a social phenomenon, an object of global fascination. Once I got started, it was easygoing. I put together the stories the bartender had told me with the stories I already knew, and by the time Robert woke up at noon, I had written an outline for a *roman à clef*, French for a "novel of keys," a method of telling a scandalous story in which real people and situations are disguised with invented situations and names. If you have the "key," you can unlock who the characters really are.

"I figured out what you're going to do next with your life," I told a sleepy bartender when he woke around noon.

"What's that?"

"You're going to become a writer."

He gave me a funny little smile and put his arms above his head to stretch, trying to wake up. "How's that?" he asked. "You going to teach me?" He pulled down the covers to show me.

"Not that. This." I handed him the pages I had written.

"I can't do it. I don't know how."

"You're going to write a book with me about Studio."

He propped himself up in bed and began to read the proposal. His eyes widened as it sank in. He whispered a low "Wow" a few times. "That's me," he said. He tilted his head questioningly, like a dog trying to understand. "Will they kill me?" he asked.

"Yes," I said, not certain if I was joking. "But while you're alive, you get paid. Lots." I would have said anything that moment to get him to stay with me, write a book with me, write a paragraph, have sex, write another paragraph, have sex, anything to keep his adorable self near me. I said that I would split the advance with him, 50-50, just like Marjoe had done with me. I thought I was being fair-minded, but I was being a schmuck. My brain had fallen to my knees. For Robert the attraction of writing a book wasn't even the money—he was hoping the book would help kick off his belt-designing business. We spent the rest of that week in a delirium of sex, marijuana, red wine, and pizza, fussing over the proposal, adding every sordid detail the bartender could remember, with me raving over his sketches for belt buckles.

I knew the idea of a *roman à clef* coauthored by a Studio 54 bartender would tickle the publishing industry, so I called the editor of the *Intelligencer* column at *New York* magazine and told him about the book. There was an item the following week with the nonsensical headline, something like *Disco Schlepper Plans Book*, along with a photo of Robert behind the bar in a tight undershirt. It did its job. The publishing industry took note. On February 8, 1979, on the basis of a ten-page proposal, the hardcover rights for *The Club* were sold to publisher William Morrow for $25,000. They were going to pay half up front on signing, $12,750, which Robert and I would split. It was thrilling to sell the book, but again not much money and not even another payment until the book was published.

One afternoon a man called my house asking if "Bobby Cohen" was there. When I asked who was calling, he identified himself as a well-known media executive with whom I knew Robert and another bartender had a threesome involving unusual sex acts. No judgment. I handed the phone to Robert, who listened for a few seconds before hanging up. He looked stunned.

"He said he was going to have both my legs broken," Robert said, his eyes getting watery. He was frightened. I felt bad for him.

"Those guys are like gangsters," I marveled. "He's not going to have your legs broken. Who would the Velvet Mafia hire to commit such deeds? Disco Sally?"

But Robert didn't find it funny. He startled me by crying. I took him in my arms and hugged him. I reminded myself that he was just twenty years old, a lot younger emotionally, and a great deal was happening to him for which he hadn't bargained.

"Did I make a terrible mistake?" he asked.

"No, no, no," I lied, enjoying how nice it was to be hugging and consoling him. "No mistake. Nobody is going to break your legs."

However, there are many ways to kneecap people.

Sylvia Miles

One brisk February afternoon, a few days after the hard-cover rights to *The Club* had been sold, Sylvia Miles and I were strolling up Madison Avenue on one of our Saturday afternoon constitutionals. It was a sunny day, the air so fresh and crisp that Manhattan sparkled like it was in high definition. I was wearing a camel hair coat from Bergdorf's (charged), a silk muffler (charged), dark Ray-Ban sunglasses (left behind by Floyd), and my hair tousled Kennedy-style by clawing it back with my fingers so it would look windblown. As we strolled up the avenue, Sylvia and I bragged to each other about how much we loved New York in the winter, or any time of the year, for that matter. We loved New York for its culture and architecture, for its rats, crimes, and hookers. Nothing would stanch our love for the city; cold or windy streets would never stop us from our appointed rambles. "You know, you can't just run away in the winter to someplace warm," Sylvia cautioned. "You have a responsibility to the city if you're a real New Yorker," and I agreed wholeheartedly, feeling responsible for the place. I would never leave New York. The city defined me. "You know, it's not everybody that owns a townhouse in New York," she said.

Sylvia and I checked out the windows of all the fashionable shops and people-watched, watching people watching Sylvia. You couldn't miss her in that coat. She was enveloped by a fox fur coat made of cascading fox tails and a matching hat. I was with her when she bought the coat in a small town in Vermont where we'd stopped for lunch on the way to visit friends. We found an unexpectedly chic little clothing shop on Main Street with the fox coat in the window. She put it on and swirled around in front of the mirror, fox tails flying, and even though it was several thousand dollars and she was usually tight with her money, she bought it in two minutes. On the way back to the city, wearing her new coat in the car, she sang Irish lullabies to me in her whiskey voice, like the drunk old lady she played in *Farewell, My Lovely*, for which she was nominated for a best supporting actress Academy Award. She made herself drowsy singing lullabies, and she fell asleep with her chin on her chest. Listening to her snore lightly that day in the car made me somehow supremely happy. When she was good, she was very, very good; when she was bad, she was a harridan.

The first thing Sylvia ever said to me was, "So what's a nice kid like you doing in a Chinese restaurant like this?" This was at a cocktail party being given by the New York University School of the Arts for the film director John Schlesinger. His new movie, *Midnight Cowboy*, starring Jon Voight and Dustin Hoffman, was coming out in a few weeks, and Sylvia Miles played a Park Avenue floozy who has energetic sex with Jon Voight on top of a TV remote control. She played the part with such conviction that actress Maureen Stapleton remarked to a friend, "Isn't that amazing, they found a hooker and put her in this movie!"

That night in the Chinese restaurant, Sylvia drew me to her like a flying saucer beam. I told her I was a student of film at NYU and I was newly in charge of booking speakers to appear at the University's Eisner & Lubin Auditorium. I was the person who had booked Schlesinger. How I talked my way into this position is very hazy to me now, but the only speaker I ever booked was John Schlesinger. Pretty soon Sylvia was holding the collar of my sport jacket with three fingers of her left hand while in her right hand her drink came dangerously close to spilling on my arm. It was a little scary, but comical. The good part was, I realized, she was in on the joke. That was the thing about Sylvia that people missed. She was in on the joke. She had invented this character, herself. "It's me, Sylvia!" she would introduce herself, Sylvia who was a brilliant but blowsy New York actress, an authentic eccentric.

A young man at the cocktail party passed us carrying a film can. "He's John Schlesinger's boyfriend," Sylvia said, crossing her eyes comically. "Do you want to meet John Schlesinger? Maybe *you* can be the next boyfriend."

"I don't think I'm up to the job," I said.

"Now, don't get a case of the shys," she scolded. "You wanna be in the film industry, don't you?" She took me by the wrist like a child and led me to John Schlesinger, who was holding court with a group of admirers.

"This is the kid who put all this together for the school," Sylvia interrupted, pushing me forward.

Everyone turned to look at me as I busied myself fawning over Schlesinger, who looked like my Uncle Willie. "Who gets these clips?" Schlesinger asked, gesturing to the film can his boyfriend was protectively clutching. Schlesinger put one hand on my shoulder and squeezed gently. "It's worth noting that I never thought to have it written into my early contracts with film companies that I'd be able to get clips from my own films. It was sheer murder to put together and I don't want it to get lost."

That was my cue. I said that I would personally take charge of his reel of film. I would be responsible for getting it back into the grasping hands of his boyfriend when the screening was over. More so, I told him that I was familiar with the projector in the auditorium, a half-truth—I had watched while a projectionist threaded it once—and that I would personally supervise the screening. At NYU's Eisner & Lubin auditorium, after a short introduction by the dean of the school, I remotely lowered the screen on the stage and turned the projector on. There was a giant white blur, surely the director's touch in which he would pull focus and reveal what the camera was looking at, but there was a burping sound on the soundtrack as the film came out of the projector. Someone yelled, "Close the gate," and I slammed the gate shut and the film bubbled on the screen. There was outrage from the audience. Shouts and people booing, people standing in the audience looking up at the projection booth.

I was thrown out of the booth. Schlesinger was beside himself, in a fury at the front of the stage. He went to the podium and said, "Let's get somebody up there who knows what he's doing." For the rest of the clips, I sat in the last row of the theater, torn between trying to apologize or fleeing. When it was over, his producer came rushing to the back of the auditorium to find me. "Don't you dare go near John!" he shouted.

I slunk down low to take cover while Schlesinger stormed by me, but Sylvia Miles stopped. I thought she was about to say something terrible. Instead, she said, "Call me. I'm in the book."

That was Sylvia for you. She was in the telephone book and I called her. She said, "You fucked up big-time, get over it," and in the same breath she invited me to a screening. We had a good time. A few days later she called to ask me to go to a dinner party at the apartment of a woman who was once a lover of Picasso. Then she asked me to go to another screening, and an opening night, and an after-party and then a thousand nights went by in a waterfall of events and good times. We had a drink in her apartment every night before we went out. When the elevator door opened on the nineteenth floor, she was standing in the doorway of 19E, posing in her outfit for the evening, on which I was obligated to review flatteringly from down the hall, like "Safari chic!" or "Terrific boots!" The doorway of her apartment was a portal to a decoupaged shrine of memorabilia, artifacts, lobby boards, Playbills, awards, photos, yellowing newspaper clippings, awards. The floor was so covered with fanned-out Playbills that Sylvia literally had to tell you where to step. There was a sleigh bed with a mink blanket, a zebra rug, an easel, a chaise lounge, and books, books everywhere, stacks of them, every one of which she had read, many of them inscribed to her by the author. Some of the art on the walls was inscribed to her too, a pencil sketch of Sylvia by Larry Rivers, a napkin signed by Robert Rauschenberg, and a silkscreen of her by Andy Warhol silk that was a gift for Sylvia starring in his movie *Heat*. Somewhere on the walls were two letters from the Academy of Motion Picture Arts and Sciences, one informing her that she was nominated for an Academy Award for Best Supporting Actress in 1970 for her role as the Park Avenue hooker in *Midnight Cowboy*, and a second Academy Award nomination in 1976 for best supporting actress for her portrayal of a boozy fading saloon singer in *Farewell, My Lovely*.

There was a small café table with two chairs in front of a big window with one of those magnificent views of Central Park, a vast green garden laid out before us that stretched all the way to Harlem. This was where we used to sit and have a drink and talk about life before we went out. She often said things offhandedly that I would always remember: "Ordinary strife and toil are ennobling to the soul." Or, "Work is sustenance. I speak as an artist." Also, "If you ever start dating a flight attendant, I'm going to drop you." Also, "You can win the lottery and lose all the money the next day betting on the horses. Or you can fall in love for what you think is forever,

146

and the next minute they're cheating on you. But theatrical memorabilia will never desert you."

For better or for worse, in the time-honored tradition of presentable single gay men, I became a walker, a regular companion of Ms. Miles. People made fun of me, always being with Sylvia, they said it was bad for business. A walker to a lady of wealth and social standing while attending the opera or charity event is one thing, but going to every party in Manhattan with Sylvia Miles was sort of déclassé. Here's the problem. It's fun going to parties, and I liked it. She was difficult sometimes, but I liked her. She was smart and warm and Jewish. Okay, she was no Jackie Kennedy, but I was no Henry Kissinger. To me, she was a rarified part of what made Manhattan great, the sprinkles on the Maraschino cherry on the sundae, one of the city's marvelous spectrum of people.

Was there an exact moment when she had gone to too many parties? Been photographed too much? Or did it just accumulate? Or was it the time she turned a plate of food over on the head of critic John Simon because he wrote something nasty about her in a review? There was no Internet then, no instant public opinion to turn the world against you. These things took time to fester and grow. That's why it was remarkable that eventually one zinger could do so such damage to her reputation—when "Madame," the bitchy puppet of bitchy ventriloquist Wayland Flowers, uttered the line, "Sylvia Miles would go to the opening of an envelope," at a gig in Provincetown. The wisecrack—repeated ad nauseam for years to come, occasionally with Andy Warhol as the brunt of the joke—did more than a little harm to her reputation as a serious actress. The joke defined her. She was defiant. "What should I do?" she asked me. "Let them stop me from going out? Fuck 'em. Let me tell you, Henry Miller worked, went out to dinner, and went to a party every night, so don't let anybody tell you any different."

It shocked me how brutal people could be to her. Some people thought she asked for it, being at so many parties and openings, with her larger-than-life personality and quirky fashion style, but still. One night Sylvia and I were in an elevator after paying a shiva call to the family of an old Broadway actor she knew from the Actors Studio, where just as she predicted, they served excellent prune Danish. In the elevator going down, a man and his wife got on at a lower floor, took one look at her, and began to talk about Sylvia as if she weren't there.

"... The actress who goes out all the time," the wife said.

"To the opening of a party ... I think?"

"No, an envelope. She goes to the opening of a sealed envelope."

Sylvia narrowed her eyes a bit, and I was afraid for a moment that when the elevator doors opened, there would be two charred figures lying on the floor. Instead, she just stared straight ahead.

Out on the street she said, "I've become an object, not a subject." I hailed a cab on Eighth Avenue. She gave the driver the address of the next destination on the night's rounds. "Listen to me," she said. "I do have a confession to make. I once went to the opening of a delicatessen. But I heard Jackie would be there."

We had a good laugh. Years later I read she used that joke in several interviews.

The Gossip Columnist

On that brisk Saturday afternoon on our Madison Avenue stroll, Sylvia and I took a detour at East 61st Street to visit Jacques Bellini's shop off Third Avenue. While a retail customer might be fitted for a suit by Bellini's tailor in the ground-floor showroom, friends and celebrities would be invited upstairs to Bellini's atelier, where there was a small bar with a shirred silk canopy and tall stools upholstered in silk zebra stripes. Guests were offered a cappuccino, a snifter of fine brandy, or a restorative. Bellini had sad gray eyes, and a long nose, so long that when he frowned, the tip of his nose almost reached the top of his upper lip. To me he was a quintessential Frenchman, but Sylvia told me that he was really Yankel Berkowitz, and his first language was Yiddish, not French. Before he became a designer and bespoke haberdasher, he was a singer at Sammy's Roumanian restaurant on the Lower East Side, where he entertained with a midget and an accordion player. "Don't judge," was Sylvia's advice. "We all start somewhere."

In Bellini's atelier that day we found Jack Martin, the *New York Post* gossip columnist, perched on a stool, nursing an espresso. I read his column every day. There was a postage-stamp-size picture of him that ran on the top of his column that Bellini said should be captioned "actual size." He looked like a normal-size person made small. Jack Martin's column was a big deal because it ran opposite the gossip heavyweight *Page Six*. Gossip was sort of an in-thing in the seventies. It was cool. It was a way for the media tribes to send smoke signals. A way to get things noticed. A way to get yourself noticed. Everybody in the media and entertainment industries on both coasts read *Page Six*, and Jack Martin got the spillover. Bellini treated Jack with silk gloves because of boldface. Jack would put Bellini's name in boldface in his column, saying some celebrity or other was seen at his shop, true or not, and Bellini would give him a $350 cashmere scarf. Jack had enough cashmere scarves to carpet a room. "I would make a suit for him as a gift," Bellini said. "But I don't know how to cut for children."

As it would turn out, a lot of people gave Jack Martin gifts. One woman gave him an ounce bar of gold in a little velvet pouch every time her name appeared in his column. Dodi Al-Fayed flew Jack back and forth on a loop from London to Los Angeles to New York on a private jet and put him up for several months at the Pierre Hotel, where Fayed kept an apartment, in return for planting glorifying items about them, particularly in the London newspaper where Fayed had his eye on buying Harrods. People were also generous to Jack because they were afraid of him. He was mad with power, vengeful, and full of petty grudges. If Hollywood tried to create a more horrendous gossip columnist, they couldn't have done it better than Jack.

"You're the one!" he said to me. "Congratulations! I've heard a lot about *that book*. You've got a Studio 54 bartender writing it with you!"

"The bartender isn't doing the writing," Sylvia said. "The bartender is doing the sit-ups."

Jack ignored her. "What's your book called again?" Jack asked. "Oh, *The Club*? Terrible title. *Aw-fu.*"

"Well, the title isn't written in stone," I said. "In fact, nothing is written at all, so far."

"Ha ha!" He laughed, as if I had said something funny.

His eyes twinkled when he looked at me. "I'm writing a book too," he said. "About Hollywood. I'm calling it *Husbands and Other Lovers*. Don't steal the title. My agent is Mort Janklow. I hope you know who *that* is?" I knew. Everybody knew that Janklow was the holy of holies of literary agents at the time, the man who got the biggest prices for blockbusters whose client list included Pulitzer Prize–winning authors as well as schlocky writers, like Judith Krantz and Danielle Steel. "Mort's been trying to find a writer for me," Jack said. "Maybe you can help me find one?" Nudge, nudge, wink, wink. Say no more.

At this point Sylvia grew impatient with not being the center of attention. "So, Jack," she broke in, and began a recitation of her recent credits, which included *Shalimar*, a Bollywood film she made in India with Rex Harrison, in which she improbably played a master criminal, and for which she was paid over half a million dollars. Even more improbable, she was in a horror film called *The Sentinel*, in which she played a dead naked lesbian ghoul at the gateway to hell, which was in a Brooklyn brownstone, not even tongue in cheek. Jack Martin jotted down some notes on a small pad in a Louis Vuitton holder, occasionally looking at me and smiling. The moment he was able to break away from Sylvia, he asked, "Why don't we have lunch, and I can tell you more about my book?" He jotted down my phone number on his pad. When he hopped off his bar stool, he surprised me by being no taller standing up.

Once he was out the front door, Sylvia laid into me. "Don't be so flattered that he likes you," she said. "It's in his DNA to hurt people. He's the dregs of all those columnists. He used to be the gossip columnist for the *National Enquirer*, for fuck's sake."

I said I would keep my distance. It was good advice, yet

that Monday a brief item ran in Jack's column, "Actress **Sylvia Miles** at **Jacques Bellini**'s East Side boutique . . ." I felt a strange pang in my chest. A different kind of hunger and need. A craving for boldface.

The Russian Tea Room

Jack was already sitting at his regular table at the Russian Tea Room on West 57th Street next to Carnegie Hall when I arrived. The Tea Room, or the "Tea Bag," as Feiden liked to call it, was Jack's home base. Just as Walter Winchell had the same table (number 25) at the Stork Club, Jack always sat at number 3, the last bar booth on the left, next to the maître d's lectern. This way not a soul could get in or out of the place without Jack seeing them. The Russian Tea Room, with its Samovars and Christmas tinsel in the lighting fixtures, had been old news, but it was having a moment as the hottest place in town for lunch, spurred by its location next to the new New York offices of ICM, the big Hollywood talent agency. Agents, actors, movie stars, and assorted show business figures would pop through the revolving front door like it was a celebrity Pez dispenser. Petitioners would stop by Jack's booth like paying respect to Don Corleone. They'd lean in and say, "You didn't hear this from me . . ." The tattle was either puffery, for themselves or their clients, or it was revenge, spite and malice. It was alarming, but fascinating. I wasn't afraid of him because he made me feel like a confidante. Knowing him was like having a pet scorpion.

Jack explained that he lived in the guest suite of Rita Lachman's Fifth Avenue apartment. Rita was an unhinged, high-strung Hungarian with a closet full of Balenciaga gowns. She had big fake eyelashes and a lacquered helmet of hair. She was divorced from Charles Lachman, the "L" in Revlon, and she was in a crazy lawsuit over her ex-husband's will, suing his second wife, who had Rita and her daughter cut out of Lachman's will. Jack Martin planted items in his column flattering Rita's daughter and the righteousness of her contesting her father's will, and Rita returned the favor with a guest room and private bath.

"But aren't you afraid of getting sued?" he asked about *The Club*. "It's *them*. Everybody will know it's *them*. I mean, there's only one Steve Rubell, one Halston. And a lot of those people are litigious."

I told him that the editors and the legal team at William Morrow publishers were confident that people who thought they were the basis for the characters would not sue for libel, because if they sued, it was their responsibility to prove that the character in the book was indeed based on them, that they weren't coke-heads, tax evaders, or participated in ejaculation-distance contests in the basement. I had the bartender who was witness to most of this. There was also "forethought of malice," which means that you deliberately published something that's false and defamatory knowing it's untrue. I explained to Jack, "We're publishing knowing it *is* true." What a jerk I was.

Aside from the cold borscht with a dollop of sour cream and a sprinkle of caviar, the main course was the book Jack wanted to write, *Husbands and Other Lovers*. He practically had it memorized, down to the smallest detail, all the multiple plot lines. The opening set-piece was at a spectacular wedding at the Beverly Hills mansion of an ambitious young entertainment attorney to the daughter of a billionaire studio head. All the main characters in the book attended the wedding party (including the caterer, it would turn out), which was held under an enormous white and gold tent. The story spread out from there into a web of affairs, one-offs behind movie sets, check kiting, sexual peccadilloes, threesomes, transvestism, theft, studio-supplied drugs, a bit of incest, and of course, America's biggest young female star used to be a man. In *Husbands and Other Lovers*, the Santa Ana winds were making everyone crazy, although I wasn't sure why the Santa Ana winds were supposed to do that, but everybody was a little crazy in Jack's book.

"It's the perfect follow-up to *The Club*," Jack said.

That day at the Russian Tea Room it seemed sensible to write another *roman à clef*, this time with a Hollywood gossip columnist as the source. Maybe I would do a whole series of *romans à clefs*, the next one perhaps with the page of a senator, or an agent's assistant at a big talent agency. I could segue from writing *romans à clefs* to real novels; perhaps eventually I'd write the memoir of my childhood that I always promised myself I'd write. "Mort Janklow will do *anything* for me," Jack assured me. "Mort told me he could get *deep* six figures for this book. Maybe even seven, if the proposal is right." Deep six! Seven! Janklow the King! A Bloody Mary later and Jack and I shook hands. We agreed on a 50-50 split, as simple as making the deal with Marjoe at Max's five years before. (Wait, that was only five years ago?) However, the Marjoe deal was with a wayward messenger of Christ; the Jack Martin's deal was with the devil.

In a blink I went from being Sylvia Miles's walker to Jack Martin's plus-one. I went everywhere with him, at his side, him showing me off, the famous writer he pretended I was, the writer of the new hot book about Studio 54 and the writer of Jack's forthcoming book, feeding my ego a teaspoon of glucose at a time. I was alarmed but fascinated by how evil he was, when he lied, exaggerated, blackballed people, how he planted items with other columnists to avenge petty hurts and snubs. I met with him several times a week when he would tell me incredible stories about the real people on whom he bases his characters. I took notes like pearls were falling from his mouth. Among other gems, Jack told me the absurd story that he was legally married to showgirl-turned-actress Valerie Perrine so she would inherit his collection of Hockneys and Warhols. I could've pointed out that there were plenty of other ways he could enrich Perrine other than marrying her, but I didn't challenge it. "Did you go on a honeymoon?" I asked politely.

"Honeymoon?" Jack replied. "We didn't even go for lunch."

I pretended not to notice that Jack looked at me like I was a puppy up for adoption. Ironically, it was the same way I looked at Robert Jon Cohen. I wondered, why was Jack so enamored of me? I just didn't get it. I was no Calvin Klein model. I was thirty-two, he was around fifty. Maybe because nobody before me was as intrigued by Jack and the dirty art of gossip? I doubted it. There were probably plenty of cadavers under his floorboards.

We ran into Feiden at a screening, and Feiden sat next to me so we could chat, but Jack Martin was leaning in so close, he was practically in my lap. Feiden was so guarded in what he said, and it was our most boring conversation ever. Finally, when the movie was over and Jack went to the men's room, Feiden pulled me aside in the hallway. "If hanging out with Sylvia Miles was bad for business," he said, "being seen all over with Jack Martin is poison. Why don't you at least wait for *The Club* to come out before you jump into a book with this man?"

"Money."

"What did Money Janklow say?"

"I've never met Money Janklow."

"You never met your agent? Odd. Uh-oh. Here comes your coauthor," Feiden said, spotting Jack coming down the hall. "Don't count on me to visit you in social jail."

When Jack read the proposal I wrote for *Husbands and Other Lovers*, he sent me a swooning thank-you note on *New York Post* stationery: "Dear Steven: Thank you. It's really wonderful. <u>Truly</u>. Every word. Well, almost every word. As for the book......<u>Caaaaaan't wait</u>. Love Jack." Next step was to sign a collaboration agreement and schedule a meeting with Mort Janklow, to hear his plan for selling it. Jack's lawyer was drawing up the collaboration agreement, but the morning of our meeting with Janklow, he had an emergency and canceled our lunch. Then it was hard to get him to reschedule. He was in Cannes, Jack said, or St. Barths. Or at his home in the Hamptons. But did Janklow read the proposal? Jack said, "Don't push Mort Janklow."

On the phone one day I told Jack that I needed to know if *Husbands and Other Lovers* was going ahead for certain, because of financial considerations. I did not tell him about the armoire, but I did explain that there was a big lag time in the book business between when the big figures were announced until the author got paid a fraction of it, and that I was living on fumes. Jack was surprised to learn that only a dribble of the advance had reached me. He said I should meet him at the Russian Tea Room for lunch to discuss it.

The restaurant was packed as usual and people were hovering over our table waiting to be seated as we tried to talk. I ordered a Bloody Mary, of which Jack disapproved so early in the day. He said that he realized I was investing my time speculatively by writing the proposal, and he wanted to advance me $5,000. I would pay it back to him when we got the book advance from the publisher. He reached into his jacket pocket and produced a meticulously written check made out to me for $5,000 from an account at a Wells Fargo Bank in Los Angeles. He folded the check in half and put it on the table between us. People waiting in the line for the maître d' were discreetly watching now that a check had appeared. "This money is a loan against the advance," Jack reasoned. "It will take the financial pressure off you," he said.

And tie me to him forever. "It's awfully kind of you, but I can't do that," I said. "I'm touched that you offered, but I've never borrowed money from anybody my whole life. Okay, my parents, but I can't take that money from you."

"*Oh yes you can,*" he sang, getting a teeny steamed. "Listen to me. I don't need the money. Anyway, it's an *advance*, and if we don't sell the book, it will be your fee for writing the proposal and I'll still own the rights. Take it. Don't make a big deal."

I looked at the check. There was a million years of bad karma in the ink. However, if he was willing to advance $5,000 out of his own pocket, it was proof that he was serious about the deal. "And did Mort Janklow read the proposal?" I asked.

"I'll call him right after lunch," Jack said.

I picked up the check, folded it in half, and put it into my pocket.

"Thank Christ our lord," Jack announced, clapping his hands together. He laughed and looked like a happy gnome. "Now, why don't you put some food into your stomach instead of Bloody Marys."

Half an hour later, just as I was finishing my pirozhki, Jack said, "I have another surprise for you that you'll really like."

"Oh?"

"Ann-Margret and her husband, Roger Smith, have invited you and me to Las Vegas to see her new show at Caesar's Palace. On *their* dime."

Incomprehensible to me. What was he thinking? Was this what the $5,000 was for?

"They're old friends of mine," Jack continued. "I told them about you writing my book and they want to meet you. They're *so* darling. Down to earth. They have *wonderful* show business stories to tell that we can use in the book. Ann-Margret's been doing her nightclub act in Vegas for years, and they're *so* rich. They offered to fly us to Vegas first class and put us up in a suite at Caesar's Palace."

"Jack, I'm not going to Vegas with you." I took the $5,000 check from my breast pocket and put it back on the table.

His face flushed red. From behind clenched teeth he hissed, "You don't have to give the check back. I wasn't paying you to go to Vegas with me. I thought you'd be thrilled to spend the weekend with Ann-Margret."

God, give me the strength and good sense to the leave the fucking check on the table and get up and go and never look back. Instead, I put the check in my wallet and shook Jack's hand. "This is an advance which I will pay back when we sell the book," I said. "However, I will never go to Las Vegas with you. But I hope you have a wonderful time and call when you get back."

I stood up to leave. He called after me, "Oh, come on now . . ."

I went directly to my bank and deposited the check, half expecting Jack to put a stop on it. He didn't.

The next morning Rita Lachman found Jack on the bathroom floor of the maid's room, too groggy on sleeping pills to wake up. She had to load him into a taxi to take him to Dr. Bobby, who gave him intravenous hydration. Jack swore he wasn't trying to kill himself. He just drank too much at Elaine's and took too many pills by accident. But I knew it was because he gave me $5,000 and I wouldn't go to Vegas with him. The question was, did I have my price?

Kansas

I didn't hear from Jack for several weeks until he called and said, "You won't go to Vegas with me, but will you go to Beekman Place? With Andy Warhol? We're going to Mark Goodson's birthday party and then out for dinner. Andy said I should invite you."

I promised myself that under no circumstances was I ever going to socialize with Jack again. Even Warhol couldn't get me out of the house. But Mark Goodson? "Mark Goodson, the producer of *What's My Line?*" I asked.

"Yes, that's the one," Jack said smugly. "I remembered *What's My Line?* was your favorite childhood TV show, you once told me."

True. I was devoted to it. Some kids watched the *Lone Ranger* or pledged themselves to a sports team; my team was the panel on *What's My Line?* Every Sunday night at 10:30 PM, with my father snoring in the bedroom, my mother in a housedress, and me in my pajamas, I dimmed the living room lights and drew close to the TV set to peer into another world. A world that was courtly and polite and clever. How it made me ache. *What's My Line?* was a simple parlor game in which the panel had to guess a contestant's occupation, like a woman who drove a garbage truck or a man who sold dynamite. Every night there was a celebrity guest—big stars like Bob Hope or Elizabeth Taylor—and the panelists were blindfolded. It was terribly glamorous. The men on the panel wore dark jackets and black bow ties, and the women dressed in cocktail dresses or evening gowns, over which my mother and I oohed or aahed. All the famous people seemed to know each other. Everybody was coming from the theater or some marvelous party or going to a nightclub. My mother and I loved the charming actress Arlene Francis, who wore a trademark diamond heart every week, and her husband and frequent co-panelist, the diminutive Martin Gabel. We didn't like columnist Dorothy Kilgallen, who seemed snippy and always asked name-dropping questions like, "Did I see you at Truman Capote's party last week?" My mother's big crush was the erudite Bennett Cerf, the publisher who owned Random House books and had a home in Mount Kisco, as did Arlene and Martin. Bennett and Arlene had sons the same age, and they were both going to Harvard. The sons of celebrities. Harvard. How it made me ache. The producer of the show, Mark Goodson, was the owner of a game show universe, which included *The Price Is Right*, *I've Got a Secret*, *Password*, and *Family Feud*. I wanted to go to his party, to tell him how important *What's My Line?* was to me, and probably to thousands of other young people who were getting their first glimpse into the glamour of New York. Maybe some of the panelists were still alive? Possibly one of the panelists would be at his party.

"Andy said you could be my plus-one," Jack said.

"*Your* plus-one?" I sputtered. "Jack, you've only been in New York a year, I've known Andy—"

"Okay, okay, let's not get into a pissing contest over who knows Andy Warhol longer," he said. "You should come. Mort Janklow is going to be there, and it would be a good time to introduce you. Andy's car is picking me up in front of Rita's building at seven. Will you meet me here?"

Janklow. A perfect way to meet him, at a very chic party, arriving with Andy Warhol. But I didn't want to be waiting with Jack in front of Rita Lachman's building when Andy's car pulled up; it would look too much like I was his date. I lied and said I was driving in from Brooklyn and that when Andy's limousine arrived to pick up Jack, I would already be waiting in front of the building in my beat-up car and follow Andy's limousine to One Beekman Place, where Goodson lived. "That's ridiculous," Jack said. "Why do you have to make everything so difficult?"

In the constellation of Warhol's acquaintances, I was in the Van Allen belt. Since I'd first met Warhol watching *Trash* at the Factory with Tennessee Williams and Bob Feiden, my relationship with Warhol was mostly a jumble of dinners in restaurants with fifteen other people, shared rides to parties in limos and taxis, Studio 54 buddies ("Oh, hi, you look fabulous."), a dinner or two at Elaine's, and a day as his guest at the 1979 U.S. Open, where the crowds in the stands stared at Warhol almost as much as they watched the volleys between McEnroe and Gerulaitis. The scrutiny I felt sitting next to Warhol was so intense that I couldn't wait for the match to be over.

I was also sitting next to him in an art gallery at an opening of his "Space Fruit" exhibit when he asked if it was really true that I tried to kill myself when I was fifteen. I rolled up my left sleeve and showed him the scar. He let out a little gasp of excitement. "Do you want to sign it?" I asked. He was thrilled. He took out a felt tip black marker, drew a line across the white scar, and then signed it. I was thrilled. Just by drawing a line over the scar and signing it, he had created a unique work of art. It was a very valuable signature but only while it was on my wrist. I thought better of cutting off my arm and putting it up for auction, and I showered with a plastic bag over my left hand for nearly two weeks. I was sad to watch it fade.

Probably my most intimate moment with Warhol, if you want to call it that, was at a party in the loft of an interior designer who lived off Washington Square. Like many nights of that lost decade, I did not know why or how I was there. Neither did Warhol, I surmised. The unusual suspects and Warhol parasites had assembled, and a small group of them, including me, broke off from the rest of the guests and took over the master bedroom, locking the door behind us. People sat on the floor or on the bed and soon a vial of restorative with a spoon was passed around.

Photographer Christopher Makos decided we should play a game he named "Would you kiss Andy Warhol's ass?" Makos, who was Warhol's court jester and *agent provocateur*, knew that Andy would be mortified by a discussion of his behind, but Andy loved being humiliated, so he sat on the edge of the bed expressionless, saying nothing while Makos went around the room, demanding to know, would we or wouldn't we kiss Andy's ass? Most people equivocated. When Makos called on me, I said, "I would kiss Andy's ass, but he already has so many people kissing his ass, he probably wouldn't even notice I was there." This was a big hit with the coke-high room. Warhol himself was so entertained that he repeated it to everyone he saw on our travels the rest of the night, but like the game "telephone," where the message gets garbled every time it's repeated, the story morphed into how I said I would perform analingus on Andy and brag about it.

The night of Goodson's party I was double-parked in front of Rita Lachman's building in my dented green Chevette when Andy's limousine pulled up. Jack came scurrying out the front door and without giving me so much as a glance, he rushed to Andy's car before the limo driver even had a chance to get out and open the car door for him. I followed them to One Beekman Place, where there was a long line of cars and drivers waiting for guests who were at the party. I parked in an illegal spot in front of the building and the doorman was furious with me. He demanded I move the car, or he would call the police and have it ticketed and towed away. When Andy and his cadre alighted from his car and greeted me, the doorman's attitude changed. I told him that if the police came, he should buzz upstairs and I would move the car. I tried to offer him a five-dollar bill, but he refused it.

Jack looked me up and down and rolled his eyes at my attire. "Oh, please, Steven, *really*?" I was wearing cowboy boots, jeans, and a double-breasted Bill Blass navy blue sports jacket with gold buttons. Andy was dressed in black tie and jeans, as were his little army of mini-Andys, who chittered away to each other. Andy didn't seem to care how I was dressed. We all squished tightly into one small, wood-paneled elevator, standing so close that I could see the net of Andy's wig where he pasted it onto his scalp.

The elevator door opened directly into Goodson's foyer and instantly I was at a cocktail party in a Broadway show. The forty or so guests in the big living room turned to look at us and chatter was suspended in midair. Behind them was a row of French doors with a spectacular view of the East River. There was a man playing Rodgers and Hart tunes on a black grand piano with a finish so shiny, it reflected the three strands of lights on the arches of the 59th Street Bridge outside the windows like a mirror. This was the moment in the Broadway show when the cast would break into the "Hello, Mr. Warhol" number, but in another second the whole room resumed what they were doing without missing a nonchalant beat. Mark Goodson stepped forward from the crowd to greet us. He was a small, spotless man who looked like he was put into a rock tumbler and polished till all his edges were smooth. Aside from an introduction as "Jack's friend, 'Steve' Gaines," he paid zero attention to me.

I tried to initiate a short exchange by saying, "Happy Birthday," so I could talk to him about *What's My Line?*, but he cut me off.

"It's not my birthday," he said with a cold smile. "But good wishes are welcome on any day." Never did I feel more miserable or a fool, I thought.

"You told me it was his birthday!" I whispered to Jack, who looked up at the ceiling like an exasperated little leprechaun. He was gaslighting me. I accepted a glass of champagne from a passing waiter and guzzled it down to steady myself. I followed Andy and Jack and Goodson through the room, smiling as I went by other guests, searching for the panel of *What's My Line?* But not one of them was there. I was hoping somebody would say, "Hi! Who are you? You're a new face around Mark's parties," but nobody smiled back.

I lost track of Jack and Andy when suddenly before me was Mort Janklow in rapt conversation with Norman Mailer. I mapped Mailer's face like a paint-by-number canvas. I remembered when I was a young teen reading *Esquire*, Mailer wrote that the most honorable thing a homosexual man could do was to not act on his impulses. It was a judgment that encouraged me to deny myself when I was a teenager. I wanted to ask Mailer if he thought differently now. At first I stood a respectful distance from the two men, waiting for the right moment to step up and introduce myself, but they steadfastly ignored me. I could hear Janklow use the manly word "penetrate." When I took a step closer, Janklow turned his back, closing ranks.

That felt bad. I backed away and took another flute of champagne from the tray of a passing waiter and asked where the bathroom was. He directed me toward a wide hallway off the entrance foyer. This paneled passage turned out to be the gallery of Goodson's private art collection. The riches of TV game shows hung on Beekman Place walls. There was a Picasso, one by Bacon, a Giacometti sculpture on a plinth called *Woman of Venice VI*, and Kandinsky's masterpiece of which I had only seen photographs, *Violet Dominant No. 603*, one of my favorite names of any painting. What satisfaction did Goodson feel looking at *Violet Dominant* in his bathrobe?

At the far end of the hall, there was an open door that led to Goodson's study. It was a dignified room, spotless like Goodson, not a paper or file in sight. The party noise was distant. There were floor-to-ceiling barrister bookcases filled with aged, leather-bound books, either the collection of a bibliophile or window dressing to fill up the empty shelves. On one of the shelves there were three Emmy Awards from the 1950s for *What's My Line?* There was also a sterling silver tray of chocolate truffles on a sideboard facing the window with the same divine view of the East River and the 59th Street Bridge as in the living room. I took a truffle from the tray and the sudden richness of the cocoa made me let out a small, ecstatic sob. I hardly swallowed the first piece when I greedily took another. Just as I was about to take a third, Andy and his cortège appeared in the doorway. My hands were full of chocolate truffles, which I guiltily stuck in my jeans' pockets.

"Oh, hi! There you are," Andy said, sounding like he'd just found a prize in a Cracker Jack box.

"Hi, Andy," I said, trying to swallow the rich chocolate without choking. "I was just wandering around and I found this beautiful study."

I suggested Andy try the truffles and he said, "No, I break out."

Andy got down to business, as Cupid, I guess he thought. Or maybe to curry Jack's favor, who knows? He was Andy Warhol, for God's sake, why would he have to court a two-penny columnist? Boldface? Andy needed boldface like I needed a second head. Andy said, "Gee, you know, Jack is just so crazy about you."

I rolled my eyes. Andy and Jack had obviously had a conversation about me in the car. Well, it *was* a little arch that I was following them in my beat-up Chevette. "I'm not encouraging Jack," I said. "Let me ask you something. Why me? Why not some Studio 54 busboy? I don't understand what the big attraction is."

"Honestly, neither do I," Andy said with a straight face. I laughed. "Five thousand dollars is a lot of money," he added.

What? My adrenaline rocketed so fast, my head nearly blew off my neck. "*Of course* Jack had to tell you that," I said angrily. "No, he didn't *give* me five thousand dollars; it's from the advance on the book. An advance on the advance."

"Too complicated," Andy said. "You should just let him blow you."

"I could never stay hard."

"How would he know the difference?" Andy asked.

We both had a good laugh at this. Once more, I tried to capture the moment and let it sink in, this paneled study, this peculiar conversation, this Queensboro Bridge and the white caps on the river, the paleness of Andy's face and the fact that he was pimping for a tiny gossip columnist, me knowing that someday this was the story I would be telling, not about chatting with the literary giants in the living room.

There was throat clearing from Andy's minions to alert him that Jack himself had appeared in the doorway, smiling from ear to ear. "My, my, my," Jack said in that annoying singsong voice he used when he thought he was being coy. His face glowed with anticipation. Had the geisha been auctioned off? Had he won? "What's happening here?" he asked.

"We're just enjoying the delicious truffles," I said. "Have one."

"I don't eat chocolate," Jack said. "It makes me break out."

I looked at Jack and Jack looked at me and we both looked at Andy and nobody spoke. I could not wait to get out of that room. I was so angry with Jack for telling Andy about the $5,000 that it crossed my mind that I should pee on Jack's shoes and walk away. Instead, I said that I was sorry but I had to leave early because the champagne had given me a headache, and anyway my car was blocking the entrance to the building.

"You're leaving?" Jack whined. "But Andy is taking us all out to dinner at Tavern on the Green."

"Actually, I'm going to find Mort Janklow first."

"Oh, I wouldn't do that," Jack said, rushing after me.

I wended my way through the guests and found Janklow just where I'd left him, except this time I walked right up to him, interrupting his conversation with a man who I later found out was John Updike. "Excuse me, Mort," I said heartily, extending my hand. "I'm Steven Gaines. I've been trying to reach you. Have you read the proposal for *Husbands and Other Lovers*?"

Janklow, furious and red-faced, announced *basso profundo*, "Steven Gaines, you can move to Kansas." What? Kansas? Updike looked affronted. Janklow turned his back to me.

I saw Jack and Andy waiting in the foyer at the front door. I asked Jack, "What did he mean, I can 'move to Kansas'?"

"I think he told you to go fuck yourself," Andy said.

I guess that was the end of *Husbands and Other Lovers*.

There was an item two days later in Jack's column about the party. Among the guests in boldface at Goodson's penthouse were **Andy Warhol**, **John Updike**, **George Plimpton**, **Bess Myerson**, **Ed Koch**, and **Steven Gaines**. A friend phoned me to laugh at it. "Which name doesn't belong on that list?" he asked. I had been to the boldface meadows of the Elysian Fields and I was told to move to Kansas.

Got Tu Go Disco

The charming con man Jerry Brandt sidled up next to me at the center bar of Studio 54 and gave me a wide smile that showed off his many teeth. "Watch this," he said. He nodded hello to a beautiful South American woman in a short black dress standing on the other side of him, waiting to get the bartender's attention and order a drink. "Give me twenty dollars," he said to her, beaming, like it was the start of a magic trick. The woman smiled back; perhaps she knew she was being conned, but she seemed cool about it. After all, this was Studio 54. She pulled a twenty out of her silver disco purse and handed it to Brandt. "What are you drinking?" he asked her. She said scotch and soda. Brandt called to a busy bartender, "Hey, Tommy, two scotch and sodas." The bartender immediately tended to Brandt, who paid with the twenty and left the change for Tommy as a tip. Then Brandt took one of the drinks, toasted the woman, and walked away. The woman laughed and couldn't wait to tell her friends. "I don't like to rape people," he told me. "I start at the ankles and work my way up."

Brandt's latest project was coincidentally about a discotheque. He was producing a Broadway show egregiously titled *Got Tu Go Disco*. This venture followed a repertoire of failed projects with other people's money. There was a rock star, Jobriath, who Brandt said was going to premiere at the Paris Opera House; a psychedelic nightclub on St. Mark's Place, the Electric Circus, which he was too stoned to find on opening night; and the French Jean Store, which sold blue jeans not necessarily French and deliberately sized too small. All of it, somehow, someway, went down the drain, the money gone. By his own account, he had lost $5 million of other people's money. Now it was *Got Tu Go Disco*. Brandt claimed he had raised $200,000 seed money for *Got Tu Go Disco* from Casablanca Records, the company that distributed the Village People records (and Dennis Parker's "Like An Eagle").

Brandt asked if I wanted to take a shot at writing the script for *Got Tu Go Disco*. I knew nothing about writing a script for a Broadway musical, which is a craft unto itself. Yet when I told Marjoe I could write a book about a child Pentecostal minister, I had never written a book. I agreed to write *Got Tu Go Disco*, whatever it was. We never talked about money because with Brandt it was all pie in the sky. The next night he took me to a celebratory dinner at Sardi's along with the show's director, Joe Eula, a fashion illustrator who had never directed anything before, and the show's choreographer, who had never choreographed anything before. We all four had the same lack of credentials. We ate and drank and talked about Brandt's grand ideas. He was fixated on a pool of water on-stage that somehow flipped toward the audience but didn't get them wet. I didn't understand what purpose it served in a show about a discotheque, but I made a note to include it in the script. The choreographer said he had to make a phone call and went to find the pay phone. A few minutes later, Eula said he had to visit the men's room, and a few minutes after that, Brandt said he would find out where Eula and the choreographer had gone. When none of them returned, the waiter presented me with the check and I realized I was had. When I saw them the next day, they thought it was hilarious.

There was a backers' audition. However, there was no score, no music, no script, just "The Box." Brandt kept on saying that *Got Tu Go Disco* was an "experience," and to simulate what the show would be like, he paid a set and lighting designer $100,000 to build a huge wooden box that filled almost an entire room of a penthouse apartment Brandt had rented on the Upper East Side. To get into The Box, you had to crawl underneath on your hands and knees and sit on a piano stool with your head sticking up into what was the tenth row of a puppet-sized theater. It was like sitting in a big doll-house with tin foil walls. A brief light show ensued of Christmas tree lights with faulty wiring, and a pretend stage production was introduced that had crude hand puppets singing and dancing. The finale was a demonstration of special effects, all climaxing when a "swimming pool" of water somehow flipped forward toward the audience, reproduced in The Box with an aquarium that unfortunately sometimes would over-flip and drench the poor soul trapped inside The Box. "That's what I meant by immersive," Brandt said. A surprising number of people crawled into The Box, including actress Ali MacGraw, but not a penny was raised.

After The Box fiasco, Brandt went silent. Then I read in the *New York Times* that I had been fired, replaced by a writer who was reportedly a former monk. I was deliriously happy. It struck me that the story of Jerry Brandt using other people's money to produce a Broadway show that didn't really exist was well worth writing about, and John Berendt, at the time the editor of *New York* magazine, gave me an assignment to recount my experiences. Brandt was thrilled to be written about in *New York* magazine and he gave me unfettered access to the production.

What I found was startling. The set designers had covered the interior of the walls of the Minskoff Theatre in Mylar sheeting, attempting to make the whole theater into a disco. No one seemed to be in charge. There were people walking around briskly like something important was happening, but nothing was happening. Joe Eula had a cocaine-induced nervous breakdown and was recuperating at home, so there was no director. Several choreographers had been hired and fired, the script was thrown out, the male "star" had been fired and a narrator substituted. The idea was being floated that the show's plot should be changed to "Cinderella goes to a discotheque." Onstage they were trying to install what looked like an above-ground swimming pool on a gimbal, a lawsuit in the making. There was a mirrored disco ball hanging from the ceiling as big as a Volkswagen, but they couldn't get it to spin.

Amid the ongoing confusion and uncertainty, Jerry Brandt sat in the orchestra and watched, a big smile on his face. He was the calmest person there. One afternoon he walked me outside into the street and standing under the marquee of *Got Tu Go Disco* with his name on it, he blithely told me that some of the investors backing the musical were under investigation for allegedly stashing $100 million in marijuana money in an offshore bank. These investors had already been arrested by federal investigators at a birthday party given for Halston, attended by Warhol, William Paley, and Steve Rubell. It turned out that Brandt got as much as $1 million in backing for *Got Tu Go Disco* from accounts in an offshore bank. Brandt told me all this knowing I would print it, but I guess he figured that if *Got Tu Go Disco* was going down in flames, he would fan the fire and bask in its glow. As he said, "When other people fall, they fall off the curb. When I fall, it's from a high wire with no net."

The article I wrote for *New York* magazine, "Got Tu Go Hustle: Presenting the Grand Man," ran in the June 25, 1979, issue. Jack Martin broke the story in his column with the headline *Mag Bares Shady Angels Behind Disco Show.* Jerry Brandt *loved* the article. Loved it. Although it stripped him bare, called him a grifter and swindler, he was high on publicity. It wasn't good publicity, but this was the seventies. The people who were less happy with the article were the investors who were being investigated by the Organized Crime Strike Force. I had divulged where they might have their $100 million stashed and how it could be traced. They were crazy angry. I figured it came with the territory; if I was going to write about drug money in a Broadway show, there'd be consequences. It was Damon Runyon and all that crap. But when the magazine hit the newsstands, I got a phone call from a man with a rough voice. "Is this Steve Gaines?" he whispered. "You're a dead man. You're gonna find your brains on the sidewalk in front of your house." He hung up. That was chilling. The first thing I thought was that he knew that I lived in a house, not an apartment. But that was silly. They probably knew exactly where I was—just look for the townhouse with the Greta Garbo plaque.

I was told by the editors at *New York* magazine that I had to report the threat to the Organized Crime Strike Force, so I called the detective who was handling the case. I told him I had been threatened with my brains outside my head and he said, "Is that so?" I could hear him taking another bite of his tuna salad sandwich before we hung up. I never heard from him again. In any event, not wanting to be blasé about my brains on the sidewalk, I decided to skip town.

Desire in Green Mountains

I called the bartender formerly known as Bobby Cohen, now known as Robert Jon Cohen, the highly paid author, and asked him to come with me to Vermont. I had friends who had a big farmhouse outside of Manchester, where we could hide for the rest of the summer while I finished writing *The Club*. It would be a steamy summer, him and me in a big old farmhouse, the aging writer (thirty-two) and the stud (twenty-one), like a Tennessee Williams play, *Desire in Green Mountains*. Robert said he wouldn't go to Vermont unless he could take his motorcycle, so I rented a U-Haul trailer, loaded Robert's motorcycle into it, and hightailed it to Manchester without telling anybody where we were going. The farmhouse was shuttered, and we opened all the windows and swept away the dust and made burgers on a rusty grill we found in the backyard.

Vermont was hot and sticky, nary a breeze, but the air smelled clean, like freshly dug earth, and there were endless fluttering things in the fields and as many fireflies as there were stars at night. I felt lackadaisical, and I tried to imitate Marlene Dietrich singing "Lazy Afternoon" to Robert to share the mood I was in, but he didn't get it. By the second week in Vermont he was broodingly quiet, troubled by what was happening to him. He didn't like hearing he was banned from Studio 54, but what did he expect? He felt trapped in the secluded farmhouse.

Living with Robert was a beautiful kind of hell. He wandered around drinking protein shakes that dripped off his chin onto his bare chest. He set up a makeshift gym on the lawn about twenty feet away from the screened-in porch where I wrote, and he did chin-ups on boards nailed to tree branches. When he wasn't lifting weights, he "took the sun," as he called it, lazing on a sheet on the lawn, slathered in Bain de Soleil, the outline of his cock visible in his navy blue Speedo bathing suit. Lolita to my Humbert Humbert. He never read a book or a newspaper while taking the sun. Instead, he listened to disco music on his Walkman earphones with his eyes closed. "*We are family*," he sang to himself, a lyric from the Sister Sledge song, "*I got all my sisters with me*." Once, he went to the other side of a big oak tree not a hundred feet from the house and I could tell by his shadow that he was masturbating. We slept in different rooms.

One still afternoon, Robert and I explored a narrow, overgrown path behind the house to see where it went. He had his shirt off and he was mopey as usual. We walked a long way without saying a word. I looked up at the sky. Not a cloud. Before long we came upon a copse of pines, behind which was an abandoned, weather-beaten shack, with a rusted lock on the door. We looked through the broken windows and poked around outside for a few minutes, then Robert turned away from me, unbuttoned his fly, and urinated in the dirt. I watched, still as a deer, until he was buttoning up, then I came up behind him and softly kissed the nape of his neck.

"Hey," he said, spinning around and pushing me away playfully. I pushed back playfully, and before I knew it, things went from playful to play-wrestling, or perhaps even more serious wrestling, and now fighting. He slapped me, hard, on the side of my head. "*Stop that!*" I yelled. I was scared of him. "What's wrong, Robert?" He grabbed me by my shoulders and threw me on the ground, knocking the air out of me. He sat squarely on my chest, pinning my arms over my head by the wrists, sneering down at me. This is the moment in the story where the hot young bartender picks up a nearby rock and bashes in the head of the older lecherous writer, by whom he feels exploited, or in the gay version the bartender kisses the writer because he realizes it's true love and they end up having barn-burning sex. Neither. Robert Jon Cohen held me pinned to the ground. I stopped struggling and went limp, trying to catch my breath. "God, you're strong," I said. "Okay, Robert, that's enough. You slapped me hard. Let me up."

"No."

I squirmed to get out from under him. He held me fast. "Robert, let me go."

"No."

I welled up out of frustration, and although I wasn't really crying, tears rolled down my face. I bent my right hand forward and managed to grab the watchband of his Rolex Oyster, his prized possession, and began to twist the wristband. "Let me go or I'll break it!" I warned. I twisted it more, bending it, and finally he let me go. I lay there breathing heavily while he stood up and walked away, examining his watch. I had ruined the band. I stayed lying down in the scruffy grass for a long time, trying to compose myself, afraid to go back to the farmhouse. A while later I could hear the snarl of Robert's motorcycle turning over, followed by a squeal as it peeled away from the farmhouse, the growl of the engine getting fainter as it disappeared down the road. It took him only twenty minutes to pack and leave. It was a long way back by motorcycle.

Robert Jon Cohen spent the rest of the summer in New York and Fire Island enjoying his nefarious fame as a freshly minted gay celebrity. He was the bartender who fucked tabloid royalty. We rarely spoke until the book was published, and when we did, we bickered. We had a photo taken together for the back cover by the great photographer Lynn Goldsmith, but Robert Jon Cohen refused to use it because the bulge in his jeans was too prominent, and he thought it made him look like a piece of meat. I spent the rest of the summer alone in Vermont, writing *The Club*, staring blankly at the piece of wood Robert Jon Cohen had nailed to the tree to do pull-ups. I went out there once to try it, just for the hell of it, but I fell and broke the big toe on my right foot.

Yes, I did find my brains outside my head that summer. The whole charm of a *roman à clef* is in the cleverness with which the writer imbues in his characters the traits or quirks or situation of the person upon which they're based. Ultimately, the writer of the *roman à clef* wants the reader to be titillated but kept guessing. Clearly, I was writing *The Club* with a Studio 54 bartender, and there was no doubt who the characters were anyway, so I went way overboard. The main character was a singer, "Jacky with a Y," whose mother was a great movie star who drank and drugged herself to death and now haunts her daughter's dressing room. Her best pal, fashion designer "Ellison," and his Latin American boyfriend, "Raoul," were always feuding high on cocaine. And so on. In the middle of all this, there was a sexy but innocent, bisexual Studio 54 bartender from Miami Beach named "Bobby Cassidy."

Magic Tapes

In June 1979, just as Robert Jon Cohen and I fled to Vermont, Steve Rubell and Ian Schrager were indicted on charges of $2.5 million tax evasion. Rubell brought it on himself. In an act of hubris, he bragged to a reporter that "only the Mafia made more money." The Internal Revenue Service raided Studio 54 and found a trove of incriminating records, receipts, cocaine, and even a list of celebrities who were given party favors. The response in New York was pure schadenfreude. Rubell and Schrager pleaded guilty, but they dropped a dime on other New York nightclub owners in exchange for federal prosecutors agreeing to drop the charges of obstruction of justice and conspiracy. They were still sentenced to three and a half years, to be spent in a cushy federal prison camp on Maxwell Air Force Base in Montgomery, Alabama. (Two movies every night, dietary needs accommodated, grounds are manicured.) Alas, in New York State you can't be a felon and hold a liquor license, so Rubell and Schrager were forced to sell Studio 54. The beginning of the 1980s would start with the end of one of the great symbols of recklessness and hedonism of the 1970s.

With Rubell and Schrager heading to prison, Morrow upped their first printing to 50,000, and moved the publication date to January 1980, forcing them to "crash out" the book at great expense. The next thrilling moment was when Bantam bought the paperback rights from Morrow for $125,000. Robert Jon Cohen and I were euphoric. Everyone thought I was rolling in dough. So did I for a quick minute, but I learned that a writer's share of the big numbers doesn't filter down for years, if it filters down at all. The hardcover publisher, William Morrow, had to get paid back their $25,000 advance, plus they got another 50 percent cut from the paperback sale, and even that amount was paid in pieces, so much on publication, so much six months after publication. Ironically, while the book was the talk of the town, they paid us *zero*.

It was a tough time to be broke again, waiting for *The Club* to be published. It was bitter cold that winter, more ferocious snowstorms than any winter since records were kept. The snow shut the city down every few days and I was in heaven. Nothing to do, nowhere to go (pre-Internet). The only sound was the muffled scrape of snowplows clearing the streets on Sixth Avenue. It was during one of those big snowstorms that I first heard the homeless man's voice calling out in the dark, and it sounded almost biblical. A prophecy.

When you live street level in Manhattan, especially across from St. Vincent's Hospital, you hear a lot of sounds, pieces of conversation of people walking by, horns and music from open car windows. But this sound was different. I heard it again, a minute or so later, closer. A deep bass voice, clear and strong, intoning what now sounded like a couplet. When it happened for a third time, even louder, I peeked out the living room windows and saw across the street that a homeless man had climbed over the wrought iron fence of St. Vincent's Hospital and was standing on the iron grating of a hot air exhaust from the hospital's laundry. He was tall and bearded, wearing a tattered overcoat and a knitted cap. He was rocking back and forth in an effort to stay warm, or perhaps masturbating. This time when he called out, I could clearly hear what he was saying: "*I'm gonna grind that pussy to a dick.*"

It turned out that the man across the street would repeat

this phrase perhaps fifty times a night, a mantra, before he disappeared at daybreak. His nighttime chanting became a nocturne of the city. "*I'm gonna grind that pussy to a dick.*" His sonorous voice echoed up and down 11th Street at three in the morning, "*I'm gonna grind that pussy to a dick.*" Sometimes he said the phrase in a rhythm, as if it were a poem or lyrics to a song. There were times when the same words are repeated over and over until they become meaningless, just sounds.

I never called the police, but the neighbors did, and also the hospital, because he was waking up patients. St. Vincent's sent a security guard to shoo him away, but he would be back in an hour. The police would take the man to a shelter, and in a few hours he was back again. I heard the words "*I'm gonna grind that pussy to a dick*" in my sleep and it was in my head all day, like an earworm. Maintenance men from St. Vincent's Hospital appeared one day and wrapped the bars of the hot air grating with barbed wire. When the homeless man arrived that night and saw what they had done to his bed, he cursed and shouted at the sky. He found a piece of cardboard to put on top of the barbs, but they pierced through when he lay down. He left in the middle of the night, defeated. I saw him several times over the next few days, coming by to check on his old home. Finally, someone, a vigilante for the homeless, I guess, climbed over the fence in the middle of the night and cut the barbed wire off. The man returned and we all lived with his presence that gloomy winter. His chant was nasty and harsh and strangely honest.

I was in bed watching television one night when a shadow came to life and scurried across the floor. The next day I found droppings, and that night the shadow came to visit again. It was a brown rat, about eight inches long, not including its tail. The city was full of them. I threw my shoe at it, missed by a mile, and it ran behind my closet door, but I still could see its beady little eyes in the dark. I thought at first it was the same rat as the night before, but more likely it was one of many rats. The rusticated basement beneath me had cracks in the brick foundation that led directly to the city vaults under the streets. In the winter the basement was a great deal warmer for the rats than the sewers, and I began to hear gnawing inside the walls at night, rats trying to find a way in. I bought steel wool and stuffed it in the cracks, but still there were rats, and the man chanting across the street. It was Manhattan.

The day after Christmas, on a night so icy only a fool would venture outside, I bundled up and went for a drink at some hellhole of a sex club in the Meatpacking District. I went for sex and I went to punish myself. This club was truly the ninth circle of homosexuality, where people are punished by gnawing on each other's necks. You had to be a little drunk and high to appreciate the ambience. At least they weren't playing Christmas carols. It was surprisingly busy that night. I spent most of my time glued against a wall holding a beer, watching the bizarre parade of participants, brushing away hands that reached out to touch me. Someone nearby lit a cigarette, and in the light from the brief burst of flame I saw that there was handwriting on the wall. It was written in pencil in a neat script just big enough to fit on a postcard, and formatted like verse. It must have taken time to write it so carefully. Who would write on the dirty wall of a sex bar in a dark place where it would never be seen? Well, I saw it. I went to get a book of matches from the bartender, but when I returned to where I had been standing, someone else had taken the spot. It was next to impossible to get him to move, and I didn't want to tell him about the writing on the wall because I didn't want him to read it, so I stood next to him stubbornly until he moved on.

I leaned in close and lit a match:

Play back the magic tapes.
Back to where this began.
Reexamine what this meant.
If you remember, then begin again.

What are the magic tapes? Maybe it's the memory of everything we've ever done, the only complete record of our lives, everything we've seen through our eyes, all of it on a tape somewhere, in our brains, and we should play it back to where this began. This what? This life was a misunderstanding, an undertaking, not organic to my soul. I lit another match and reread it. How can you begin again? If things happen the way they're supposed to, right here is where I belong, with a match reading graffiti in this cold and empty night. There is no way to begin again. It's all a Möbius strip, an Escher graphic. This sleazy bar. That stupid book. This gay life. I should have another drink before I walk home.

Liz Smith

The following day, December 27, 1979, Andy Warhol wrote in his diary, "We got sent (an advance) copy of Steven Gaines's book *The Club*, the 'novel' about Studio 54, and it has a chic Seventh Avenue designer named (laughs) 'Ellison,' who works in the Olympic Tower and has a Peruvian boyfriend named 'Raoul.' The names are so bad." Unable to contain his glee, Warhol called me. "I don't know how you're going to get away with it," he said, breathy and thrilled.

I didn't get away with it. The consequences of publishing *The Club* were like being run over by a very long locomotive. The first car doesn't kill you; neither does the last. It just keeps you wondering what hit you and when it will stop. The book shipped to bookstores nationwide in January 1980 and it was not well received. It got some space in the gossip columns, but the book wasn't the clever commentary for which one hoped. I had an opportunity to comment on café society in New York City in the 1970s and I blew it. Late morning of Tuesday, February 5, 1980, the day after Rubell's farewell party at Studio 54 before he went to prison, which of course I did not attend, the telephone woke me. "I thought I would hear from you," Jack Martin sang, oh so chipper. "Haven't you read Liz Smith yet?"

"No, why? I asked sleepily.

"Why? My darling, you are *in* it. You *are* it. You're the lead item. Liz is nationally syndicated, too. *Greaaat* exposure. Anyway, it's awful, all those lawsuits," he said.

"Lawsuits?" Completely awake now.

"Lawsuits galore! Do you want me to read her column to you?" He was gleeful, that little prick.

"Yes. No! No! I'm going to the newsstand and I'll call you back."

I threw a coat over my pajamas, and in my Guccis with the holes in the soles, I trudged through the slush on 11th Street to buy the *Daily News*. I spread it out on the dining room table. There it was, the headline of Liz Smith's column, *"The Club": Celebs think it goes too far.* It read, *"There are a few famous people who are not writers, but these glittering ones think that they know when enough is enough. Liza Minnelli, Halston, Bianca Jagger and the now jailed owner of Studio 54, Steve Rubell, are all said to be contemplating suits against authors Steve Gaines and Robert Jon Cohen over their new roman à clef from Morrow, titled 'The Club.' The celebrities feel that the book is more clef than roman. . . . Liza, Halston, Bianca, Steve and their friends feel 'The Club' set in a disco resembling Studio 54 defames them beyond belief by using the all-too familiar basis of their fame, their lives, their looks, their backgrounds and their personalities to create characters in the novel. And these characters come off in the book as pretty unsavory, indulging in various machinations, payoffs, sex, drugs and carryings on that do indeed seem to go beyond the pale. Halston, the elegant and darling dresser of millions of women has already turned his complaint over to the Norton Simon attorneys who help run his big design empire."*

I sank into a chair. Lawsuits? Norton Simon attorneys? They have billions. Probably they would say I hurt his brand, but they'd still have to prove he was Ellison. I started to reread the column when the phone rang. It was Ellis Amburn, the editor at Morrow. "We haven't been served with any lawsuits," he said. "Have you?"

"Reading Liz Smith's column was the first I heard of it. I wonder why she didn't call me for comment before publishing it?"

"It's causing quite a bit of stir here at Morrow," Ellis said. "They're very unhappy here to read all this in Liz Smith's column."

"Ellis, you told me that the lawyers said nobody would sue because the burden is on the plaintiff to show that the character was based on them, but they weren't coked up all the time, when they were."

"Any one of those people could sue us for any reason," he said. "They can sue us next week or in a year if they want to. Sometimes they send a letter of intent, saying they're going to sue, and they don't. It's too soon to know. But if they send a letter of intent, our insuance company comes into it and we have to freeze any payments to you."

"Oh no. I *need that money, Ellis.* I expected that money."

"I know. I know. None of us are very happy about this. Listen to me and remain calm. There's more. The paperback publisher, Bantam, is delaying their first payment to us, to make sure they aren't buying themselves into a lawsuit."

"Ellis, all this terrible stuff is happening, and no one knows if the lawsuits are true."

"We'll have to wait until this blows over, keep our heads down. If I was you," Ellis said, "I'd call Liz Smith and ask her where she got her goddamn information. Ask is it true or is she just saber-rattling for them? She published it, she should know where it came from."

I tried to compose myself and dialed Liz Smith. "I expected you'd call," she said in her Texas drawl. I always liked Liz Smith; she seemed honest and fair. A stand-up Texas blonde.

"I wish you had called me before you published that column," I said, my voice shaky. I tried to keep composed, but I was on the verge of crying.

"You know that's not the way it works," she said.

I didn't know anything of the sort. She could have called me for comment. I asked if she could at least tell me where she got the information about the lawsuits. "You know better than to ask for sources, you're a journalist."

I thought, *Lady, you wrote something that's deeply affecting my life in a negative way.* I told her the source didn't matter, but we *needed to know if the lawsuits were real.* It was causing all sorts of trouble with the publisher, but we hadn't heard a thing from Norton Simon or anybody. Her column said that Norton Simon was getting involved. Was she certain?

Ignoring my plaint, she uttered words about which I have often thought: "You have to be philosophical about what comes next." What comes next? Was she prophesizing my extinction? She continued, "With some people there's a time in their lives when they decide to straighten up and fly right and stop all the drugs and alcohol and wild living."

What? Drugs and alcohol? That wasn't my story. Wild living? What did any of that have to do with *The Club*? What was she talking about? Like the crack of a whip in my head, it dawned on me. Jack Martin told her there were lawsuits. Revenge. I once told him about what our legal strategy was. "Was it Jack Martin who told you about lawsuits?"

"Steve, you know better than that." She hung up on me.

Jack. I was trembling so hard trying to call Jack that I could hardly press the buttons on the telephone. Rita Lachman answered and said he had already left for the Russian Tea Room. Now I was hurtling down the track. I called Mort Janklow's office and demanded to speak with him. I was surprised when his secretary put me through. I guess getting to speak to King

Janklow was a perk of being the headline story in Liz Smith. He said, "What is it?"

I said, "You can go fuck yourself in Kansas."

There was silence. I said, "Hello? Hello? Did you hear what I said?" Then I realized he had already hung up on me.

Three people had hung up on me and it was barely noon.

I took a big swig of red wine from a bottle that was still sitting on the table from dinner two nights before, and a few more for courage, and in another five minutes I was out the door, my hair wild, dressed in whatever clothes were handy, my cashmere coat with a torn pocket hanging down. I hailed a taxi to the Russian Tea Room and burst through the revolving door. Jack looked stricken to see me stalking toward his table. The place was jammed and noisy, but not so noisy that you couldn't hear me screaming at Jack all the way in the back of the restaurant, where people stood up to see what the commotion was. I called him every childish name I could think of, including midget and faggot and liar, but why go on? I said nothing witty and bright or smart. It was just name-calling. "You called Liz Smith!" I shouted.

Jack looked calmly at me. "Have you had lunch?" he asked.

Wise ass. I turned and stormed out the door onto busy 57th Street. It was freezing cold and I wasn't wearing socks. What did I just do? I didn't want to go back to West 11th Street because I was so paranoid, I thought the police might be looking for me for causing a disturbance in the Russian Tea Room. I imagined cameramen running down the street taking pictures of me, strobes flashing. I needed to hide. Sanctuary. The quiet room in Payne Whitney, a shot of chlorpromazine every six hours, a padded room with three squares, and no armoire.

I hailed a cab and told the driver to take me to Payne Whitney. I don't know if I thought I was going to commit myself or what. I didn't feel suicidal, unless you call wanting to take sleeping pills in a snowy forest and let the animals eat me suicidal. Does making a scene in a restaurant qualify? Multiple lawsuits? They certainly didn't take reservation for the quiet room, if such a thing still even existed. I'll never be welcomed back to the Russian Tea Room again. The cab turned down East 68th Street onto the long driveway of New York Hospital and pulled up in front of the Gothic doors to Payne Whitney Psychiatric Clinic. As soon as I walked in, I was calmed by the warm, dry heat of old-fashioned radiators and the smell of furniture polish and dignity. A receptionist behind a glass partition asked if she could help me.

"I'm an alumnus," I said, making her smile.

"Recent?" she asked.

"Naw, class of nineteen sixty-two. Eighteen years ago. I was feeling nostalgic, and I thought I'd drop in to have a look-see." I could tell by her expression that she was going to tell me it was against the rules to have ex-patients have a look-see, so I added, "I just want to sit in the lobby. I'm having an anxiety attack and I need to compose myself."

In that case, she said, I could visit.

The lobby was like the library of a venerable Ivy League university club, dignified and quiet, with old-fashioned leather sofas and high-backed armchairs. Above the fireplace there was a portrait of William Payne Whitney, serious, unsmiling, his hair parted down the middle. No one knows for certain what led him to donate $10 million to build a psychiatric clinic in 1932, but I could see in his eyes something unsettled. Underneath his portrait there was brass plaque with an inscription, acknowledging "... the wisdom and generosity of Payne Whitney who established this ... house for the healing of the sick and troubled ..."

Upstairs the sick and troubled must be quite different from

what they were in 1962, when I was in residence. It was no longer a club of wealthy neurasthenics. No mulligatawny soup served with dinner. Were there any Broadway producers and heiresses and architects up there today? I doubted it. There was health insurance now, you didn't have to be rich to be there, and there were more recovering alcoholics and junkies in Payne Whitney than crazy people. I left this place when I was fifteen years old with the absolute belief that one day I could be a panelist on *What's My Line?* And now what? Writing gossip books. Making scenes in restaurants. Unrequited love affairs. This wasn't how I'd planned it, but no one to blame but myself. Freud said there were no accidents. I designed the life I was living through thousands of little and big choices. Or not. "Vanity of vanities, all is vanity," Solomon said in Ecclesiastes when there was no boldface. "Everything is utterly meaningless! Only vanity drives us forward."

I took a deep breath of Payne Whitney air and thanked the receptionist at the front door for the booster shot.

"You know they're tearing this building down and building a new wing?" she asked.

"I didn't know," I said, feeling terribly sad. I was glad I had a moment to say goodbye. "It will bury a lot of stories and hope and sadness with it."

Laguna, London, Long Island

Reporters were calling me from all over the world about *The Club*. They only wanted to hear nasty stuff about Studio 54 and the lawsuits. Global schadenfreude. My phone rang continuously until I shut it off. Truth be told, I yanked the wire out of the wall. The first person to get through when I had the phone reconnected was Feiden. He was not easy about the whole book fiasco. He told me it was a Pyrrhic victory, and that while I managed to embarrass those people, their lives went on untouched, but my career was in ashes, and that when Rubell gets out of jail everybody will love him again, but they'll never forgive me. "You don't have fame, you have ignominy. Maybe you should give up writing for a while?"

"Or maybe I should dig in deeper," I said. "You know, like when you're in a riptide you swim farther out to escape."

After that, Feiden put me into social jail.

One night I took Sylvia to Chinatown, where the streets looked shiny and wet and smoke was coming out of the manholes like it did in film *noir*. We walked around and around until she found a basement restaurant that she said had the best wide noodles in all of Chinatown, but they tasted their very best at one in the morning with other cast members after a performance in an off-Broadway play in the 1950s. I understood. I told her I loved memories like that. I had moments filed away to relive. I wanted to remember that night with her at the Chinese restaurant. I asked her if she thought I had ruined my career, like Feiden said I did.

"Don't ever let anybody try to tell you that you have to sleep in the bed you made," she said, eating a noodle in oyster sauce. "There are thousands of people who were written off and bounced back bigger than before. But to do that you must teach yourself to be brave. You must pull yourself up by your bootstraps every day of your life. What you should do now that you've got so many people angry with you is to go away, move to Europe or somewhere, pretend you're Truman Capote or Noël Coward, move to an island off the coast of Greece, write a bestseller, then come back and everybody will love you again."

"That simple?"

"That's not so simple," she said. "The hardest part is moving away."

"But won't you miss me?"

"Naw, I'll just pretend you moved to California."

Ironically, I moved to California. A month after the release of *The Club*, Peter Brown called. Peter was a former president of the Robert Stigwood Organization, the British entertainment company about which I had coined the phrase "Velvet Mafia." Previously he was an executive with NEMS, the Beatles's management company. He arranged for John Lennon and Yoko Ono's wedding and was immortalized in John Lennon's lyrics *"Peter Brown called to say, 'You can make it OK, you can get married in Gibraltar near Spain'"* from "The Ballad of John and Yoko." Peter had been closemouthed about the Beatles, part of the Liverpool clan's code of *omertà*. But now he wanted to write a tell-all book about "the boys," as he called them. He asked me if I would move to Laguna Beach to write the proposal. He had a three-bedroom apartment on a bluff overlooking the ocean and offered one of the bedrooms to me while I wrote. He read my recent press and was unperturbed by it. I was on the next plane.

When I arrived in Laguna Beach, I discovered that Peter was going through what he would later call his "Lost Weekend," several years of champagne, beach, and boys. I was lucky enough to catch him on the tail end of it. Laguna was like Lourdes for me. Its coves and beaches were as untouched as any Southern California town could still be by 1980, and many locals were vestiges of a community of local artists and surfers and aging hippies from the sixties. Shortly after I arrived, Peter arranged for me to have lunch with a wealthy, aspiring movie producer, Tomas D'Sandro, who lived in Emerald Bay, a private community up a rocky hillside with dizzying views of the ocean. Tomas had also read my recent concerning press, but because my name was in boldface, he was impressed.

Tomas asked me to write a script based on an idea he had about teenagers and video games, with an ice-skating sequence, which sounded as strangely out of place as Jerry Brandt's flipping swimming pool. Peter Brown negotiated a $25,000 fee up front and the man wrote a check, no contract, nothing. It was a miracle: $25,000 fell into my lap. The next day I dressed in tie and jacket to open an account at a local Laguna bank to deposit the money. Peter laughed at me when I left the apartment. I asked him what was so amusing, and he said, "You'll see."

When I got to the bank, I was the only one wearing a tie and jacket. Everyone else was wearing Ocean Pacific shorts or baggies and T-shirts. Welcome to endless summer.

The first thing I did with the money was send a check for $5,000 to Jack Martin, but he never deposited it. The second thing was to remotely empty the armoire and pay off all my bills. Every morning I ran on the beach like New York was chasing me, but instead of dodging the armoire, I was trying to avoid the sea lions sunning in the coves. I bought a camera and took hundreds of pictures in Laguna, trying to capture the moment, including a selfie every day at sunset.

I spent the next few months writing the Beatles proposal on a rented IBM Selectric, seated at a large round dining room table overlooking the coastline. I consulted legal documents that Peter Brown had kept in his possession for decades. I named the book *The Love You Make.* At the end of summer 1980, I moved to London and rented a rambling flat near the British Museum. Peter told everyone that he was writing a book about the 1960s and I was his "writer." He introduced me to the Beatles and their inner circle and took me into their homes. I was able to have on-the-record conversations and conduct taped interviews that were personal, revealing, and often blunt. I met Paul, George, and Ringo, their families, friends, and business associates. It was unimaginable that John Lennon would be murdered on December 8, 1980, shortly after I'd finished the interviews, except for one, Yoko Ono, who spoke with me the coming spring.

It was a gift to be able to tell the Beatles's story. It was a magnificent story, sprawling and complicated, intertwining their business, creative, and personal lives into a narrative populated with oversized personalities in starring roles. *The Love You Make* was on the *New York Times* bestseller list for fifteen weeks in 1983. It became the largest-selling biography about the Beatles worldwide, with over 500,000 copies in print.

The success of *The Love You Make* did not make me a hero. Hardly. People were still furious with me for writing, *The Club*, and it only pissed them off more when I bounced back with a bestseller. As it would turn out I wrote other books that would piss off people. I put the notion of forgiveness and salvation in my rumination folder, along with the underwear Miracle Marvin saw on my bedroom floor, and whether or not the lawsuits over *The Club* were real or Jack Martin just made it up, or if Janklow ever really said *Husbands and Other Lovers* would bring seven figures.

A little reality gratification goes a long way to quelling any desire to be seen in gossip columns. I'd rather be in the book review than *Page Six,* although I love *Page Six.* These days everybody gets bold face for fifteen minutes.

Many people in this story are dead. Jack was fired from the *New York Post* for taking payola and moved back to Los Angeles. He died a suicide in his house on Dick Street in West Hollywood in 2016. Three hundred empty vials of cocaine were found. Halston died of AIDS, as did Steve Rubell. So did Robert Jon Cohen, Jacques Morali, and Dennis Parker. My friend and Greek Chorus, Bob Feiden, died of AIDS-related illness in 1993. Tinkerbell committed suicide by jumping out of a fifth-story window. Jerry Brandt died of COVID. There's no trace of Floyd the Outlaw on the Internet. I've kept track of Topher. He found the love of his life, a burly, hairy person who has the lips of a gorilla. Last I heard from Topher, they married and were wine merchants, living in the Napa Valley. He sent me a picture, and he was nearly bald. Miracle Marvin lived until he was eighty-three. Sylvia Miles passed away in 2019 at age ninety-four with $2 million in the bank.

I've learned only two things for certain: Freud was wrong, you can find lust and love in the same person, and Sylvia was right, you do not have to sleep in the bed you made. The last part of Sylvia's recipe for redemption was for me to say goodbye to New York City in earnest. They warned Virginia Woolf that the city overstimulated her. In any event, the writing on the wall said, "reexamine what this meant, then begin again."

I sold the Greta Garbo Home in 1990. It was heartbreaking, like putting down a beloved old dog. I cried sitting on the front stoop, unscrewing the brass plaque that now sits on a small easel in the living room of my home in Long Island. The

Hamptons are beautiful, the beaches calm and restorative when the summer people are gone. The ether really does sparkle in East Hampton, the way the artists say it does. It's been a wonderful place in which to live and write, but I still exist under a cloud of what the Welsh call hiraeth, a deep sadness and longing for places and people who have disappeared or died. The Jews say that each person is a cemetery for the dead, we hold them inside us, and they are alive in our memories. After I sold the Greta Garbo Home, I could never walk down 11th Street again. I couldn't bear to look at it. I know the ghosts of the people who wander through its rooms. I might have left it alive, but my ghost is there, too.

About the Author

Steven Gaines is the twice *New York Times* best-selling author of *Philistines at the Hedgerow: Passion and Property in the Hamptons* and *The Love You Make*. He has also written *Marjoe*, the biography of evangelist Marjoe Gortner; *Me, Alice*, the autobiography of rock star Alice Cooper; *The Love You Make: An Insider's Story of the Beatles* (with Peter Brown); *Heroes and Villains: The True Story of the Beach Boys*; *Simply Halston: The Untold Story*; *Obsession: The Lives and Times of Calvin Klein*; *The Sky's the Limit: Passion and Property in Manhattan*; *Fool's Paradise: Players, Poseurs, and the Culture of Excess in South Beach*; a memoir *One of These Things First*; and the novels *The Club* and *Another Runner in the Night*.